MEMORIES OF THE UNEXPECTED

TO MS. COLLEEN SECOR

The Story of a Tuskegee Airman

GOD BLESS
REV MILTON HOLME

Copyright © 2013 by Milton L. Holmes

All rights reserved. No part of this book may be reproduced or utilized in any form or by any means, electronic or mechanical, including photocopying and recording, or by an information storage and retrieval system, without written permission from the author.

ISBN 978-0-9891940-0-6

Printed in the United States of America

This book is dedicated to my family, past and present.

ACKNOWLEDGEMENTS

I appreciate Mark Kemp, former president of the Hannibal Cox Chapter of the Tuskegee Airmen, New Jersey, who personally ensured that I attended the Inauguration in 2009 of our first African-American president, Barack Obama. The next month, Mark, along with Dr. Larry Nunley, Community Outreach Liaison with the president of the Baltimore City Council's Office, presented me with the Congressional Gold Medal at my eighty-third birthday celebration.

My thanks extend to Bob Ballard, who paved the way for me to attend the Prince George's County Presidential Committee Inaugural Ball, one of the most important events in my life.

Special thanks to Sharon Hunter-Nikalaus, president of the Hannibal Cox Chapter of the Tuskegee Airmen, for her tenacity in promoting the work and recognition of the Documented Original Tuskegee Airmen (DOTAs).

I am deeply touched by the encouragement, dedication, and countless hours my daughter, Janet, worked with me on telling my story. She and graphic designer, Noah Urban, were instrumental in preparing the manuscript for publication.

I have the deepest appreciation for my editor, Tony Bruno, retired New Jersey Administrative Law Judge, who envisioned this book even before I put pen to hand. As members of the Tinton Falls New Jersey Rotary Club, we have developed a spirit of mutual respect.

I'm blessed to have as a consultant and organizer, Dr. Josephine O'Neal, who guided me through this project with exceptional skills.

Most importantly, I thank my wife, Jackie, who has kept me somewhat steady in the many unexpected detours we have experienced.

To God be the glory.

FOREWORD

When Reverend Doctor Holmes asked me to read and editorially comment on his autobiography, I was both surprised and honored. Our acquaintance was limited to Tuesday morning Rotary Club meetings; our conversations centered on books we had read and current events. Our backgrounds were strikingly different; one might say we grew up in segregated communities, mine white, his black. Our votes would likely cancel each other's. None of this, though, lessened my interest in his story. It only brought me to the realization of God's presence in our meeting.

Former President George H. W. Bush spoke of a brilliant diversity spread like stars, the thousand points of light. Doctor Holmes will give me the "glare" as I refer to him as one of those thousand points. However, his lifetime accomplishments on behalf of the people he has served, the segregated, the oppressed, the financially and educationally deprived, justify my conclusion. Doctor Holmes demonstrates why he is proudly a member of Tom Brokaw's "Greatest Generation," an American born shortly before the Wall Street bust, growing through the pains of the Great Depression, and volunteering to serve in the military of his country, enduring the pains of military service in the deep South.

Reverend Holmes shows himself as the example of his beloved Rotary's motto of "Service Above Self," as he tells his story in the same manner and with the same words as he speaks: blunt, to the point, no holds barred, what you see is what you get. Clearly, an outstanding intellect, qualified for many positions of personal gain that he passed on in order to afford the opportunity to his soul brother. Using his God-given talents for his enrichment would have been more profitable but would have been totally out of character.

On a more personal note, as an alumnus of the University of Notre Dame, I am reminded of the words of our Victory March: "What, though the odds be great or small, old Notre Dame will win over all." Reverend Holmes explains how, no matter how great the odds, he "won over all."

Several are the origins of the nickname, "Fightin' Irish." The one I ascribe to is the proud spirit of the Irish in the times when they were discriminated against, to fight back, and to overcome prejudice with gritty determination and hard work. Reverend Holmes has demonstrated that spirit of the underdog throughout his life to overcome the obstacles of hate, discrimination, and treatment as a second class citizen.

Tony Bruno

SAVED BY GRACE

I felt my body giving up. There was nothing left for me but certain death. My primary care physician had later all but assured me that without prayers ascending to Heaven, that's surely what awaited me, an eighty-two-year-old man suffering from accidental food poisoning and confined to the Cardiac Intensive Care Unit.

I didn't have time to be sick, let alone die. The handprints on my previously intended book were all but etched and completed. I was engaged in preparing for the trip my wife, Jackie, and I were excited about taking to Tuskegee, Alabama, for the Tuskegee Airmen National Historic Site dedication, a few months away. Visiting with some of my former comrades would be exhilarating, and I couldn't wait for the journey. We had planned to pack our Acura MDX and spread our sixteen-hour destination over two days, resting midway from our New Jersey home with relatives in Windsor, Virginia.

Then, suddenly Jackie suffered a severe knee infection, resulting from what we thought was a simple slip and fall. She was rushed to the hospital when her fever climbed to almost 106 degrees. The doctor couldn't determine the root of the infection, which caused her knee to swell close to the size of a soccer ball. They realized that they would only be able to examine it by x-ray or MRI because any type of surgical procedure could risk an even deadlier toxic reaction.

So, I drove the fifteen miles to the hospital at least twice a day for the next three weeks to be by her side, returning home only for a fragmented nap here and there. I had never seen Jackie that sick before, and I was extremely overwhelmed and weary. My biggest comfort was the support I received from my sisters, brother, and daughters, who would visit from Baltimore to make sure I ate and rested. They would also accompany me to the hospital and remain there with me.

Finally, still barely able to walk, Jackie was transferred to a rehabilitation facility where she continued recovering with grueling therapy sessions. After two weeks, she returned home where the therapy and doctors' appointments continued.

Although her progress was time consuming, we finally decided to take a much needed break from the two-month-long ordeal and vacation at a nearby resort in Lancaster, Pennsylvania, with a few family members. One evening we all ate at a local outdoor seafood restaurant. We sat under a pavilion at picnic tables spread with sheets of brown construction paper and topped with bushels of steamed hard-shell blue crabs, corn-on-the-cob, and fries. A few of us ordered an additional serving of raw oysters, something I had enjoyed for decades.

The oysters were so good that I returned to the restaurant the following day with my daughter, Sheila, and her husband, Ronald. We relaxed outside with our open-shelled oysters dotted with lemon and hot sauce, and slurped down those little appetizers, chewing the slimy contents and finishing them off with refreshing cold sodas.

By the time we returned to the resort, a couple of us who had eaten oysters the previous night, had a negative reaction and ended up with stomach cramps and several trips to the bathroom. Near that day's end I was beginning to feel sluggish. The entire following day, I vomited, suffered with diarrhea, and was practically confined to bed, feeling more like a hospital patient than a vacationer. Jackie and I realized that I had to find a way to get better by the following day in order to drive those 250 miles home. But no soup, dumplings, hydrating drinks, or medication succeeded in making me stronger.

When we were ready to leave, I was so weak that my daughters had to pack my SUV and stock me with enough liquids to keep me strong enough to return home. Jackie was still restricted to limping, depending on the help of a cane; so I had the daunting task of steering us through the country resort that doubled as an RV campsite and, by the grace of God, driving us home.

Leaving all of our belongings in the car, we finally settled in our bed. I became weaker and weaker but managed to keep it from Jackie, who was absorbed with her own discomfort. Any strength I could muster to go to the bathroom on my own was given to me by God.

One of my daughters, who had been on vacation with us, called the next day to check in. Hearing my broken and raspy whisper, she panicked, hung up, and called a family friend who lived nearby. The friend arrived within minutes and climbed in through a window since neither Jackie nor I could leave the room. After some small talk, she pinched the skin on my hand into a fold. It failed to spring back, meaning it had lost its elasticity. Realizing I was completely dehydrated, she called 911, and I was rushed to the hospital. By then, I was in cardiac arrest, had little chance of survival, and was admitted to CICU.

I was heavily medicated and completely immobile. Every organ in my body felt as though it was shutting down, and I developed renal failure. Yet, although helplessness had taken control of my body, an incomprehensible peace came over me, leaving me with a resolve that I had come to my life's end.

For a moment, I opened my eyes to see several family members standing quietly around the room. Others were on the other side of the door peeking through the window. I remember thinking, "That's love. I'm at peace. I don't care if the Lord takes me."

Later, three of my grandsons, Euvon Jones, Ronald Smith Jr., Robert Moore Jr., and one of my granddaughters, Alexie Smith, visited, laid hands on me, and prayed. I gradually felt revived and made a decision that I wasn't going anywhere. I wanted more of that love.

I eventually began to rise from that dark situation to remember a similar one sixteen years ago, when I underwent an emergency quadruple bypass. My former pastor and seminary classmate visited to pray for me prior to my operation. Again, during recovery, I awakened to my family and church members waving and blowing kisses from the other side of the window. It is impossible to describe the feeling and motivation of such love, but it made me believe I would recover and complete my doctorate program, which I had begun before surgery. The following year, at age sixty-seven, I received my Doctor of Ministry degree.

Now, after miraculously recuperating from a rare strain of bacterial food poisoning that I acquired after eating contaminated oysters, a strain even my doctors could not pronounce, I was relocated to the general recovery floor, energized and ready to fight my way home. While waiting to be discharged, I was interviewed and invited to spend a week in a rehab facility to help regain my strength.

That is, until a blood clot suddenly developed in one of my legs, causing excruciating pain. After a Doppler ultrasound confirmed the clot, a surgeon informed me that because I was an old man with damaged legs and congestive heart failure, there was little chance I could survive any procedure other than amputation. I was in so much pain that I quickly agreed. But, again, God answered my prayers. The next morning, the clot was successfully removed without amputation, and my heart was stabilized. I was released from the hospital the following week and transmitted to the same rehab facility Jackie had recuperated in less than a month earlier. The insurance company would only allow me to stay one week.

Two weeks after being released from rehab, I experienced congestive heart failure again and was hospitalized for another week. Again, I was interviewed for rehab, but the insurance company refused to authorize the treatment. Within myself, I questioned the control insurance companies exercise over patient care.

My in-home recovery was a very slow process. Subsequently, another month later, I had cataracts from both eyes, as well as my gall bladder, removed. Unfortunately, I was unable to attend the dedication of the Tuskegee National Historic Site in October 2008. Thank God my disappointment was short-lived.

One week after the removal of the second cataract and forty pounds lighter, I was doggedly determined to accompany my fellow Tuskegee Airmen to the Inauguration of President Barack Obama, the nation's first African-American president. My grandson, Euvon, escorted me and handled my wheelchair for me. My pride said, "I don't want any attention on me." I refused to be treated as a cripple among many of the Airmen who, though older and more challenged, walked unassisted. I stood on my own and mingled with my former comrades. We shared experiences of post-World War II. Many of us had dedicated our lives to help improve our communities.

Though young, ambitious, and ready to protect our country, we Tuskegee Airmen embarked on a mission that was encompassed by great principles: preparation and discipline for one's self, solidarity and camaraderie, and love for everyone. These principles had fundamentally shaped my life. It was at Tuskegee that I engaged not only in arduous academic instruction, but also in teamwork and discipline. *All for one and one for all.* That concept was ingrained in us more than anything else; that we were part of a team, never striving for individual recognition. It meant that if your comrade was suffering, you were to suffer alongside him. If he was being hazed, you were to jump in and be hazed with him. In other words, in combat, you must agree to risk your life to save another. Honor was also emphasized. It was drilled in us that our word was our bond, more than a contract. My covenant of honor, integrity, and loyalty were strong points in my life. I miss that today, because those were values that should not have been sacrificed in our quest for material superiority. They should still be applicable for America and this democracy as an example for other countries.

On that icy morning in January 2009, as President Barack Obama ushered in a new era of racial harmony in America, I believed I had been blessed with everything this world had to offer, because of the love and prayers of my family and friends. That evening, my daughter and son-in-law, Janet and Euvon, accompanied Jackie and me to the Prince George's County Presidential Committee Inaugural Ball.

I realized how important it was to talk about what brought me to Tuskegee Institute and how it had fashioned my life. I embarked on a new journey to revisit the televised and other recorded interviews I had participated in over the last decade or so regarding my Tuskegee experience. I spent hours and hours with my sisters, brother, and cousins, unfolding the blanket of our heritage that had been neatly tucked away in our minds for decades. As we explored the ostracism, humiliation, yet unbounded familial love that accompanied that time, I realized I have inadvertently dedicated my life to the love of my parents, particularly, my father. He was not an educated man, yet through him I was taught the power of knowledge, honesty, and loyalty, which carried me from the small cuddled community of Turners Station, Maryland, to the spacious fields of Keesler Air Force Base in Mississippi, and ultimately, Tuskegee, Alabama. There I decided what I would do for the rest of my life. My goal was to encourage and assist others who were less fortunate, to stretch beyond their boundaries and achieve their highest potential.

In retrospect, although there were many experiences that channeled my attitude and behavior, I realized there were three experiences that have had the greatest impact on my development and character.

First, my father had demonstrated a determined protection of his family, my mother and their children, his siblings, and his in-laws.

Second, my oldest brother, Lloyd, contracted the deadly contagious disease, tuberculosis. During his lengthy illness of more than two years, and subsequent death, I was practically ostracized in my small segregated community of Turners Station, where my siblings and I were born and raised.

Third, I had been accepted for pilot training at Tuskegee Air Force Base during WWII, and soon realized that the German and Italian prisoners held in the United States had more privileges than we blacks, even though we had fought against them as well, which made me bitter and resentful.

Reinhold Niebuhr stated a belief that has also defined my attitude when he wrote, *"God, grant me the serenity to accept the things I cannot change, the courage to change the things I can, and the wisdom to know the difference."*

LETTER TO MY GRANDSON, MILTON HOLMES

October 1931

Dear Milton,

Just a few lines to let yu hear from me. I aint doing no better since yu been gone. Yu only five and a half years old, but yu stayed wit me dis summer by yusef for over a mont. Yu took good care of me. Bought me my food and water. I fell and broke my hip. Yur grand pappy cooked fore he left for work. Yu sho liked those chicken dumplins. He work on the farm all day. I hurt so bad. Aint gonna be here much longer. No doctor, no hospital, no cure. Gonna tell yu somin. Yu gotta be careful bout foke who don't care nonten bout yu.

We suppose to be free in 1889, but we still had to work the white mans farm and live in those dirt floor shacks. One night one son of Mr. Spivey cided to rape me. I only foteen years ole at de time, round the Christmas holidays. Really hurt me. Said he would beat me up if I didn't. Told me better not say a word cause dey had de right to do what they want wit they niggers. Went back to de shack and fell in Mamma's arms and cried long time. Mamma say had to be tough.

Yur daddy Joseph was born next following September 1890. He very light skinned as yu can see. Monts after yu papa born, the rapes started again. He always made me go up that dirty hay loft in de horse stable. Yu Aint Mary was born a little over year after yu papa. She very light skinned too.

Soon as I turn 18, I marry John Holmes, yur gran pappy. He very dark like me. We had six more, two aints and fore unks. Yu papa's whole sister Mary died when she roun 10. Believe from (con)sumption. We was sad. I told my girls watch de white men. Don smile or look happy. Dey married early. Jody, as u papa was called, always tried protect me, beinst de oldest, very light. Worked hard to help take care of us. He so proud. Worked from morning till night, only stopped for a few minutes fer lunch. Ate in de field. When he round 21, married a little brown skinned gal name Alice Butler. They had little girl, named her Mary, after yu papa's sister. Den had a little boy, named him Joseph, after his papa.

Guess yu papa was tryin very hard to be accepted, cause he always took up for his sisters and brothers, beinst the oldest. He loved to play guitar. Taught himself. Had a good ear. Could take all the strings off and put dem back in tune. Played so foke dance. But one Sunday morning he sent his brother Marshall walking to a friend house to bring back his guitar he lent him. Marshall started out but soon came back all beat up. He hadda pass a white church down dis dirt road, but dem white foke in the church yard beat him up, sent him back crying. Yu papa took his pocket nife and went walking down de road on the other side of de road down there hisself to get his guitar. When he got to de church, all of dem hollered, where yu think yu goin nigga? Yu papa said, none ya dam bisness. The whole church went to beat him, but he cut three of dem first. One cross the stomak, one in the throat, and one cross the nose.

Dey beat him up but dey had to let him go cause was so much blood from de guys and women was screemin. None o dem died. Yu papa scape and hid in de woods. De sheriff came to my house, tole me if Jody didn't turn hisself in, dey gonna rest me. When yu papa home and heard dat, he hitched de horse and wagon and I put on a dress wid a wide skirt. He got under my skirt in the wagon so as nobody could see him. I drove de wagon to de sheriff so he could get there without being hung.

Yu papa worked fo de judge and he sentenced him to 5 years in Richmond, Virginia penitentiary to keep him from being hung. Yu papa served 3 years and 10 monts. Twas during Worl War I. That why he missed de war. He wife d'vorced him wile he in jail.

Yu papa was discharged bout 1920, an after leaving de prison, he began workin on a job that was building a road. De whites found out who he was and dey begin talkin bout that nigga. As soon as he married yu mama in 1922, he moved to Maryland to keep from getting killed. Yu brother Lloyd born in 1923, a sister Lille Florine in 1924. She died after 6 weeks. Yu born in 1926 and yu sister Velma born in 1928. She was two in 1930. She drowned on de beach where yall was livin, several monts after yu sister Joyce Odessa was born. Yu mama had a nervous breakdown.

Yu papa's son Joseph tried to hitchhike from Virginia to see yu papa right afer that. When he almost to Washington D.C. he stop by a well ta get a drink a water and he was shot and killed. Nobody was rested for dat.

I feelin poorly now so may not see yu no more. Be good in school and take care yuself. Gain tanks yu for takin care of me.

Yurs truly,

Granma Nancy Holmes

Although the facts are accurate, the "Letter to My Grandson" was a fictitious letter written by me in February 2007, and presented at a dinner program sponsored by the Monmouth Center of World Religions and Ethical Thought (MCWRET) at the Unitarian Universalist Congregation in Lincroft, Monmouth County, New Jersey, where MCWRET held meetings and programs throughout the year. Members of the organization belonged to different religious faiths.

Each year, we would sponsor a Thanksgiving program with this congregation. The participants represented the various faiths, and each performed a selection of its choice, such as dancing, singing, or speaking.

Their objective was to improve racial and religious tolerance. In order to develop insight into the attitude and forbearance of each of us, members expressed how a family member had the strongest influence on his or her behavior.

Some participants displayed pictures and diverse mementos. The actress who read "Letter to My Grandson" was dressed in early 1900 period attire and read admirably. Several presentations left audience members in tears.

Sometime in the 1960s, decades after the actual event described in my letter, I met two of the men with whom my father had had the altercation. I was visiting my Aunt Doris at her home in Virginia. She had somewhat of a silent permission to sell food and alcohol in her home. I presume that was because she lived in the country where farms were shaded by soaring trees. Her town was centrally located, and many conveniences were miles apart.

There was an acceptable level of racial tolerance at my aunt's house, as long as people were sociable. Five of her brothers, all whose thick, bulky frames stood between 5'10" and 6'4", lived on the Joyner property, a stone's throw away. I don't think it dawned on any guest to visit for anything other than leisure and fun.

The guys, black and white, would come from their farms on the weekends, congregate in the tattered and musty living room, or sit around the adjoining dining room table that rocked slightly whenever someone shifted or rested an elbow, arm, or shot glass on it. Its sharp-tooled etchings and moisture stains absorbed into the mahogany wood had their own stories to tell. Aunt Doris was a short and rotund, quiet yet commanding mother figure; wherever she sat was the head of the table.

It was the one place enemies would temporarily become friends and socialize, sipping shots of homemade or store-bought alcohol, enjoying fried chicken wings, telling whopper stories, and laughing at each other's jokes. On this particular occasion, after realizing who I was, and in the midst of one hilarious moment, one of the men pointed to the scar on his nose and the other showed us the scar on his neck, scars my father apparently inflicted. Nothing followed but more laughter and stories.

There I learned that age does and should bring maturity and tolerance to our attitudes and behavior.

LOYALTY

I witnessed early on how loyal and fearless my father could be. When I was seven years old, Mama's seventeen-year-old brother, Tom, was embroiled in a fight with a guy in his hometown of Windsor, Virginia. Tom had been sliced on the left shoulder just above his heart. The other guy was also stabbed by Tom. He was arrested and served thirty days in jail for his involvement.

Apparently, my grandmother, Rosa Joyner, shipped Tom up north to us in Baltimore, Maryland, to escape the sheriff and receive medical treatment. My first memory of this time was of him lying on the couch in our living room bleeding from his chest. Even though it wasn't a life-threatening stab, to my young eyes it looked quite serious. My parents bandaged the wound as best they could and took him to a doctor. He stayed with us for several months, until he completely healed. Then, remaining in Baltimore, he moved in with his sister, Margie, and got a job.

A tradition in Mama's family was that every year, she and her eleven siblings celebrated Grandma Joyner's July twelfth birthday in Virginia. Although my parents were a little suspicious that Tom might be arrested, we went to the celebration anyway. Word did circulate, however, that Grandma Joyner's children would be around for her birthday this particular summer.

My older brother, Lloyd, and I always looked forward to that time. Grandma Joyner had a very large yard for all kinds of games, including climbing trees and swinging from their limbs to see who could jump the furthest.

We also shot marbles, played croquet, horseshoes, and softball. The ball was made out of rags stuffed into one of my grandmother's old stockings, and a tree limb served as the bat. We always had plenty of smoked ham, fried chicken, greens, potato salad, and desserts like homemade ice cream and cake.

Two of my younger uncles, Hyde and June, were working on a broken car window in the front yard, while the rest of the family mingled, catching up on old and new family news. All of a sudden, we noticed an unfamiliar car looming down the Lane. The Lane was a dirt road about a 500-yard stretch between one major thoroughfare and The House, our name for Grandma Joyner's spacious white home, the only one on the fifty acres of Joyner property. The only way in and out was through the Lane.

When the vehicle got near enough to be recognized as a sheriff's car, Hyde and June jumped in their car and sped past the sheriff to buy some shotgun shells. We children were left wondering what was going on.

Sheriff Whitehead pulled up and, leaving his deputy inside to guard the car, jumped out asking questions about Uncle Tom. Everyone just looked at or past him, peaceful and quiet, except for my uncles, Jasper and Thaddeus. Their on-your-mark stance and clenched fists showed they were ready to rumble. When he didn't get the cooperation he was hoping for, the sheriff made his way up the stairs to the porch. Uncle Leslie stepped in front of him, blocking the entrance to the house. Leslie was a big-boned 6'5" hustler who'd shoot you before he could get a good look at you.

"You not goin' in my mama's house without a warrant," was all he said.

"I don't need no warrant."

Officer Whitehead reached for his gun. Daddy leaped up on the porch behind him, close enough to give him a shave. We had no idea what he was going to do. I was shocked at his fearlessness. Leslie, realizing that, in fact, the officer had no right to go in the house and that he was protected, ran to his bedroom and got his shotgun, but there were no shells. This was in southern Virginia, where hanging blacks was no problem. There was zero tolerance for a sassy Negro. Blacks were not supposed to look at a white man in the eye without saying, "Yes, Sir" or "No, Sir."

The deputy in the car started yelling, "Come on, man. Let's get out of here. Let's get out of here!"

The sheriff made a quick glance around the living room, sidestepped down the porch steps while pointing a suspicious look at each man. He slid into the car and before he could get both feet inside, the deputy spun around, and drove back down the Lane. Hyde and June were returning from the store with their shells. As they leisurely passed the sheriff, their cars got close enough to keep from driving into the ditch on either side.

Luckily, Tom had climbed through his bedroom window where he had been resting, sneaked into the woods, and ran to another farm that was barely within view.

When given the "all clear" sign, my cousin, Russell, and I darted around the back and ran toward the farm where we found Tom walking with his friend as he was plowing the field. They were just talking small talk, never mentioning that the sheriff had come looking for him. We told him that the sheriff had gone.

Tom never got caught, but a year or so later, he voluntarily turned himself in and served his mandatory thirty days in jail. As soon as he was released, he relocated back to Baltimore and worked for the Baltimore Gas and Electric Company during WWII. After the war, he returned to Windsor, married, and built a home on a two-acre lot. He worked on the family farm and raised his own family there.

Lloyd and I were proud of Daddy because, although he weighed no more than 150 pounds, to us he was a giant. He always protected his family, regardless of the circumstances.

FIVE PRINCIPLES

In 1937, the world was on the brink of World War II. Dr. Addison V. Pinkney was my seventh grade teacher at the time. He taught us about what the war would mean for our country, as well as potential international alliances, using several references to World War I. He mentioned that during the first war, the draft eligibility ranged from eighteen to forty-five years of age.

I knew Daddy was born in 1890 to a black woman who had been raped by a white man whose last name was Spivey. He had a younger sister by the same man, but she died before she turned ten. Both were very fair-skinned. Years later, his mother married a black man named John Holmes and had six more children, who were very dark. By the start of WWI, blacks were being drafted and Daddy was certainly eligible, yet he had never discussed the war nor his participation in it. He told me some aspects of his life as a young man, particularly his work ethic, his guitar playing, and his limited education, but mentioned nothing about the war until I asked him why he never talked about it.

He told me the story my grandmother described in the imaginary letter I wrote about how he became a convict in the penal system. Daddy was living in Virginia and married to his first wife, Alice. They had two small children, Joseph and Mary. One particular day in 1916, he had loaned his guitar to a friend who wanted to play it at a party that Saturday night. The next morning, he sent his younger half-brother, Marshall, to retrieve the instrument from his friend. Well, his brother had to walk past a white church, and as he did, some of its members ran out and beat him, sending him home, injured and bleeding.

Daddy said he sharpened his pocket knife, slipped it in his back pocket and walked down the dirt road on the opposite side of that same church. By this time, services were over, and one white guy standing outside on the lawn yelled at him.

"Nigger, where do you think you're going?"

"None of your damn business," Daddy retorted.

Three of the guys raced across the dirt road, snatched up some tree limbs along the way, and grabbed Daddy, kicking and beating him. Before they knew what happened, he had sliced one boy's throat, slashed another one across the belly, and yet another one across the ear and face. The whole church was in an uproar. The women were screaming, and blood was everywhere. In all the commotion, Daddy managed to stumble away, his body covered with welts and bruises.

A short time later, the sheriff came to his home to arrest him, but he had escaped out the back and ran through the cornfield. Halfway through, he stripped off his shirt and hung it on a corn stalk. The sheriff shot it to pieces. He then realized he would have to hide out for a while, so he pitched himself in a briar patch and waited it out.

After dark, once he thought it was safe enough, he started back towards home. As he approached the house, sounds of crying and wailing swelled in the air. He rushed inside only to learn that his mother had been arrested earlier. They finally released her with a warning. If Daddy didn't turn himself in, she would be jailed. The matter was settled without further discussion. He agreed to give himself up.

The following day, his mother, Nancy, not quite 5' tall, stepped into an oversized dome-like dress, strolled outside and hitched a mule up to a buggy. Daddy was able to hide under the skirt, slide onto the buggy, and lie concealed on the floor so he could get to jail without being lynched.

Fortunately, Daddy worked for the judge he now stood in front of needing leniency. The judge also knew Mr. Spivey and, in an act of sympathy, advised Daddy that he would have to go to jail or risk certain death. He was given a five-year sentence in the Richmond penitentiary and served three years, eight months, and seventeen days.

It was difficult for Daddy in prison because, even though he was light-skinned, he was still a nigger to the white man. However, it was there that he sharpened his guitar playing skills. He constantly strummed out original melodies, and his calloused fingers played the strings like a hummingbird fluttering its wings. He told me about the train that travelled about forty-eight miles from Suffolk to Richmond. It was allegedly the longest track in the world without a curve. He wrote a song about that train. I only remember one of the many verses:

> *The longest train I've ever seen/Was on the Richmond line*
> *The engine passed at sunrise/The tail end passed at nine*

Years later, when I was a young boy, we would dance to that song for quite a while.

Although prison had its hard times, Daddy was favored with the position as the warden's cook. However, the warden was very finicky about his meals. His biscuits had to be baked to perfection and his coffee could not have one grain in it.

One morning, just as the warden sat down to eat his breakfast, he jumped up and stormed out of the room, almost knocking Daddy over in the process. Daddy inspected the coffee and spotted a lone grain swirling around the surface. Realizing his fate, he quickly eased a knife out of the drawer, leaned against the counter, and began sharpening it. The warden, in the meantime, returned with a whip pointing at three burly inmates across the hall.

"Put him over that barrel and beat him. Now!" he commanded.

Any prisoner who committed any type of offense that warranted a reprimand was usually laid over a huge barrel on his stomach and held down by two prisoners, while beaten by a third. In Daddy's section, naturally, all the prisoners were black.

Just as the men stepped toward Daddy, he took a step toward them wielding his knife. "Now, I ain't got nothing against y'all, but y'all know why I'm here, and I'm gonna send one of y'all where we all need to be. I ain't got nothin' against you, but don't put your hands on me," he warned in a decisive tone, just above a whisper.

They knew why he was incarcerated in the first place. So they backed off.

"We ain't bothering that crazy man," they told the warden.

Soon thereafter, Daddy was let out of jail to purchase some items for cooking. While at the store, he talked to the clerk about what happened earlier and how the warden had gotten kind of evil toward him. A stranger who had overheard the conversation suggested he talk with a woman who could help him. After he talked to her about the incident, she sent him to the store to buy some items. What they were he never revealed.

Daddy said he never had another problem after that. The warden soon became a little less rigid and, in a month, was gone. Even though Daddy wasn't specific, I could only surmise that the woman had invoked a little voodoo on the warden.

By the time Daddy's prison term was up, his wife had divorced him.

I admired my dad for his courage. He often told me five principles he believed in, which I have tried to live by, especially during the Civil Rights era:

1. NEVER BETRAY YOUR BUDDY

2. NEVER START A FIGHT, BUT BE PREPARED TO DEFEND YOURSELF

3. ALWAYS TELL THE TRUTH

4. ALWAYS LISTEN – YOU CAN LEARN FROM ANYONE

5. ALWAYS RESPECT A SENIOR

THE FIRST TRAGEDY

Turners Station, a slight suburb of Southeast Baltimore County, was established to provide housing, particularly for African Americans who had migrated from the South, escaping strenuous farm work and meager wages, to work in factories and steel plants.

My parents relocated from Virginia to this community, moving into a small home on Oak Street. Daddy, along with many other men in the area, worked as a laborer at a steel plant.

Bethlehem Steel, as did many large plants, built small towns around its industry, which were usually segregated. In Sparrows Point, where the plant was situated, its black employees settled on two streets of wooden row homes, similar to paltry town-homes. Whites, on the other hand, occupied neat red brick homes on the remaining twenty or so streets. Blacks had access to the company store and the post office, but were denied access to the schools. The rest of the several businesses were owned by and available to whites only.

Turners Station, located about five miles northwest of Sparrows Point, was almost geographically isolated by water on one side, railroad tracks that accommodated trains and streetcars on another, and roads on the remaining two sides. White communities surrounded those two roads to the north in other towns, such as Dundalk, Halberd, and Saint Helena, which began a mile from the edge of Turners Station, extending into Baltimore City. Actually, the Baltimore City/Baltimore County boundary line runs through St. Helena, classifying it as both a county and city town. We could drive through the roads to get to the city, but we weren't allowed to patronize any stores. While the majority of us lived in attached row homes, there were only a few of us, including my family, who lived in single-family dwellings. Each home had a 4' x 4' wooden outhouse in the backyard that served as a bathroom, since there was no sewage. Like others, we had a metal tub for bathing. Often, particularly in the winter, two or three of the children would have to be bathed in the same water.

Furthermore, a pump was available for about every eight to ten houses to retrieve water. It was especially challenging during the winter months because the pump, which would often freeze, would have to be primed, which meant a couple of cups of water would have to be poured down the pipe to thaw the frozen pump enough to access the water.

Our community was a decidedly close one with a secure connection. My family was one of about 200 residents there. Many of our leaders lived in the area and owned their own businesses, such as a couple of stores, a shoe repair shop, barber and beauty shops, a dry cleaners, and a savings and loan association. We also had our own post office, movie theater, churches, and an elementary school.

My older brother, Lloyd, and I were raised during the height of the Depression, but by then, my parents had already been immersed in difficult and traumatic circumstances. In 1923, the year following their marriage and relocation to Maryland, Lloyd was born. Mama was eighteen years old. Lilly Florine was born the following year but survived less than a month. Then, in 1926, I was born, and my sister, Velda, arrived in 1928.

Daddy emphasized being a loyal team member and never betraying another. "The white man rules," he reasoned. "so just know what you have to do. Although you sometimes have to work for them, getting an education is important. They will never accept you on an equal basis, but you just keep on doing what you have to do, and get along with your own people."

Daddy's day began between five and six o'clock in the morning, with breakfast, followed by working in his garden during the summer, which provided us with fresh greens. Then he would eat a light meal and take a nap while Mama packed his lunch, always his largest meal, in that half-circle shaped bucket he carried to work for more than thirty years. It was shaped like a cylinder with upper and lower compartments. She would store his meat and bread in the upper portion, and vegetables or soup in the lower one. Daddy would go to work from three to eleven o'clock at night, eating his meal around seven or eight o'clock. When he came home, the newspaper would be waiting for him to read before retiring for the evening. Then the cycle would be repeated the next day.

With the onslaught of the Great Depression of 1929, jobs became scarce. Ultimately, unable to maintain the rent, and with three children in tow, my parents moved from Oak Street to a rental property on Edgewater Beach. It was the largest, most beautiful and popular beach for blacks in Maryland, owned by the community physician, Dr. Thomas. To supplement his income, Daddy conserved the beach grounds and, on the weekends, valet parked the guests' vehicles, while Mama sold her homemade dinners and desserts.

As little ones, my brother and I had access to the play area with the swings, a see-saw, and a sliding board. Sometimes we would sneak over near the water and sit on the ledge of the gangway near the boathouse where Doc Thomas kept his small yacht. Lloyd and I would sit on either side of the boathouse and swing our feet above the lake, even though there was some trepidation in my heart that if we fell into the water my mother would not find us in time.

Sometimes Lloyd and I would spend time with Uncle Jasper and Aunt Lettie in Baltimore City to give Mama and Daddy a break. Once, in the middle of the night, we were awakened with the news that two-year-old Velda had drowned. The next thing I vividly recall was my older cousin, Georgette, lifting me up with her hands under my arms to see my little sister laid out in a white dress in her casket. I remember hearing a lot of crying. I remember walking through the field to bury her. I have often thought about her and desired to visit her grave, but have never been able to find it. Perhaps trees and bushes have since covered the small unmarked site in Virginia.

Years later, when we were old enough to understand, we were told the story surrounding Velda's death. Mama, who was pregnant again, had been preparing dinner while Velda played outside. She engaged Mama in a game in which she would run up to the screen door and say, "Bye-bye, Mommy," laugh and run off, disappearing around the corner of the house for a few minutes.

"Okay, see you later," Mama would answer. This continued several times, until once, Velda knocked softly on the door. Mama opened it and stooped eye-level to her. "Who is it?" she asked Velda. She gave Mama a hug.

"Bye-bye, Mommy. "I'm going home now." She giggled and ran off again.

Minutes came and went when Mama noticed that Velda had not returned. She called out to her and when she didn't get a response, she went to look for her. She walked down about thirty feet to the small beach which bordered our back yard. There she saw her baby floating face down, her long wavy hair sprawled out over the water. My parents were devastated, and after Odessa was born several months later, we left the beach house and moved in with Daddy's sister and her husband, Mattie and Paul Buchman.

The Depression that began in 1929 was rough. I remember once when Uncle Paul walked about ten miles to and from a market in the city, bringing home a shopping bag half full of chicken feet so my mother could cook some chicken and dumplings.

In 1931, when I was five, my Grandma Nancy Holmes fell down the stairs in her tiny home and broke her hip. I was taken to Smithfield, Virginia, to stay with her for the summer. I would carry her meals and drinks to her once my grandfather had prepared them. Lloyd had to remain in Baltimore to work, picking fruits and vegetables for a few pennies. All I could do was sit quietly all day and wait for grandma to call me. I was extremely lonely for my brother.

When summer was over, and just after I started school, we received word that Grandma Nancy had passed. My father travelled to Virginia with Aunt Mattie and Uncle Paul. Mama was pregnant and could not go.

In the winter of 1932, Fred was born in Aunt Mattie and Uncle Paul's house. Of course, it was the custom, cost-free, and convenient in those days for babies to be birthed at home. Daddy gave me the privilege of naming him.

Shortly thereafter, we moved from Aunt Mattie and Uncle Paul's and settled into another small home a little over four blocks from the beach house. Our new home was on a street where each little house was a single dwelling with an outhouse in the back yard. By then, we were really beginning to feel the stress of the Great Depression.

THE GREAT DEPRESSION

The Depression, combined with the loss of one sister and the births of another sister and brother, was relentless in its effort to drive my parents into a fit of despair. But they were a strong force and just kept doing what they had to do. By 1934, with two deceased children, they still had four to raise.

My family had relocated within the same community three times. We were almost destitute, and food was a precious commodity. We were able, though, to raise enough chickens so we could eat one every now and again. Occasionally, we ate a little bit of ham that we brought back from the country, enough to last until our next rare trip. Beef was out of the question, and the only time we ate fish was when we went fishing. Mama made biscuits and cornbread every day, serving them with homemade peach, watermelon rind, or apple preserves. We ate generous amounts of greens and string beans picked from our garden, as well as potatoes and eggs.

Many small businesses were affected by the Depression, and staples, such as sugar, flour, and butter, were rationed. So Mama would sometimes walk Lloyd, Odessa, and me across the street to a Jewish-owned store, especially if we had no money. The owners, Miss Sadie and her husband, would let us get a few things on credit and would record the purchase in a little book, allowing us to pay it back whenever we could. Their service was prompt and efficient, and they were always kind to us.

In the summer of 1932, when I was six, Lloyd and I were sent to Windsor to work on Mama's parents' farm. Those were the days before tractors, when farmers needed as many hands as possible. Staying in the country was somewhat of a culture shock. There were no traffic signals in that dusty town with hardly any paved roads, and the few homes that were at least three blocks from the railroad tracks belonged to the whites. It was twice as rural as Turners Station, which made our community seem a bit more upscale. During that period, blacks did not live close to the center of town. All our shopping was done about a mile away from home, and we had to walk. Blacks neither owned any businesses nor worked anywhere in town. Every store, service station, bank, post office, and house within a mile was owned and operated by whites.

In early summer, along with Hyde and Alonzo, two uncles close to our age, we were each given a hoe to chop grass around the peanuts that were planted plentifully on Joyner Farm. We would also pick all the ripe corn that was ready to be eaten. Then in August, we'd pick the harder corn used to feed the chickens and pigs, and put the rest in sacks for planting the following year. We would strip the leaves, called fodder, with our hands and tie them into bundles, placing them on the corn stalks. They would be used for feeding the horses and cows during the winter.

Our days began at six-thirty in the morning. We ate breakfast and arrived in the field an hour later ready to work. At noon, we took a lunch break to eat our heaviest meal of the day. We would play ball or pitch horseshoes until three o'clock. Then we'd return to the field until six-thirty, and afterwards eat a light meal. Sometimes we'd either walk to town to purchase a few items for our grandmother or treat ourselves to a piece of candy, play for another hour or so, then off to bed. Sundays and rainy days were the best. All we did was play and rest.

Grandma Joyner, a stoic full-framed figure, was half white and half Blackfoot Indian. Her long, thick silver braid was a permanent fixture down the middle of her back, and her high cheekbones rarely broke into a smile. She held onto every nickel earned from selling peanuts. Acquiring land was the only thing that could pry her clenched fists open. At the time of her death in 1959, she had accumulated well over fifty acres of land.

Grandpop Joyner was quite the opposite. He was a short man who was so dark he looked blue. He spoke with the accent of an islander. He was such a loquacious and fun-loving person, and never worked hard on the farm. He left that to his six sons, Lloyd, and me. And he didn't seem to have a job himself because he was always nearby, leaving me to wonder how he always had money to give us. The main thing he took pride in was his watermelon patch, which we weren't allowed to go in. He kept track of who walked in the patch by the size of the footprints. I tried it once, though, not to take a watermelon, but to see if he would know. He did and I got a swift tongue lashing.

We later learned that his main occupation was making corn whiskey to market. He would venture deep into the woods and produce his homemade concoction of strong spirit to the tune of 100 proof.

A couple of years later, good ole Grandpop died. By then, Lloyd was twelve and I was nine. We couldn't travel to Windsor to pay our respects because we had to go to school. Five-year-old Odessa was in the hospital at the time with a life-threatening disease called erysipelas, an acute bacterial infection marked by fever, intense redness, and severe swelling of the skin and underlying tissues. It could appear anywhere on the body and, in her case, it attacked her face, resulting in itching and burning sensations. Today, it is easily treatable, but back then there was no penicillin or antibiotics. On their way to Virginia to attend Grandpop's funeral, Mama and Daddy stopped by Johns Hopkins Hospital so they could visit with her and donate blood for her.

By the time I was eight, we didn't have to spend all of our summers working down the country. There was enough work to be done at home. A pickup truck would stop through the neighborhood around eight o'clock in the morning for workers to pick tomatoes on white-owned farms. There were usually around ten children and at least two adults ready to work the field and earn a few pennies. Lloyd and I disliked the task because hauling a half bushel of picked tomatoes almost 100 yards to the truck was harder than anything else we had ever done.

Three times during the summer we would pick lima beans on another white man's farm not far from home. We would earn about fifty cents a week and take home a pound of beans for the family. However, the third time, usually in August, which we liked the least, the beans would be scarce, and we would have to work twice as hard just to get a few. We struggled hard to pick our typical fifty cents worth.

Those of us who worked this way were considered poor, but we didn't care. It put food in our mouths and some small change in our pockets.

MY FIRST PRAYER

One time, Mama decided to go to the field and pick some beans herself. Lloyd and I did not have to go. But before she left, she woke us and told us to eat cereal for breakfast and biscuits and preserves at lunchtime.

"All I want y'all to do today is shell that bowl of lima beans on the dining room table. I'll fix them for supper when I get home," she instructed in her usual quiet and soothing voice.

When we finally got up, we ate our cereal, moseyed over to the table, and leisurely began shelling the beans. Just as we got into a rhythm, a couple of friends walked by the house, yelled, "Ball game at one o'clock!," and kept on walking.

We knew what that meant and picked up our pace shelling those beans as fast as we could. Baseball was one of Lloyd's favorite sports, and he never missed a game. After a while we checked the clock. Any other time, the minutes would have crept by slower than a caterpillar. Now, though, they seemed to pass by like a silver bullet, and even though the game was about to start, we weren't even half done. To make matters more pressing, Lloyd was on the team that would be playing against another team from the other side of town, and he was a key player, one of the best in Turners Station. We looked at each other, flustered, and eyed the clock again, hoping the time had slowed down to its usual crawl. It had not, and a decision had to be made. Suddenly, we jumped out of those chairs, dropped the bowl of beans on the table, and dashed out the door into the summer heat. We raced to the baseball field, rationalizing that the game would be over in time for us to get back home and finish shelling those beans before Mama and Daddy got back.

Normally, the game would last a little more than two hours, but by the end of the ninth inning, the score was still tied, spilling over into another hour and a half. Lloyd's team finally won, and we were really upbeat as we sauntered toward home; so, we paid no attention to the man approaching nearby until he greeted us.

"How are you, Mister Holmeses?"

Daddy walked on past us en route to Adams Bar to buy his usual evening toddy. A sardonic grin brushed across his face. Not another word was said, and he kept on moving. We hurried home, only to find Mama cooking the beans she finished shelling, the same ones for which we had been responsible. She was sweating profusely in that hot kitchen, and we knew we were in trouble. Without acknowledging us, she whispered in an even icier tone than Daddy's greeting, "Go on out back and both of you cut three branches off that small tree that don't break and plat them right."

The small tree held thin branches that surely would bend without breaking. Those kinds of branches made the worst switches because they could welt you real good without snapping, and the moisture would make the pain even more piercing.

Lloyd and I took deliberate steps toward the tree and searched long and hard for the thickest switches, believing they would be less painful. But it seemed like all those switches had the thickness of a pin, which was not a good sign. To make matters worse, we had to bend and twist and pull, bend, twist, and pull them from the tree because they were too moist to easily snap off. When we came inside, Mama calmly showed us how to plat them and would periodically check on us to make sure we did it correctly, so they wouldn't break at the ends.

When we were done and handed Mama the switches, we were ordered upstairs to undress down to our underwear. We tried to relax, hoping beyond hope that she had forgotten our punishment. Next thing we knew, we could hear each stair-step creak with her body weight, followed by her entrance with her arm raised, ready to whip. She started with the lower legs and when they started marching in place, seeking the protection of our arms and hands, it was across the hips, then across the back, and down the legs again. Mama's short thick frame had stamina and strength, and she was unmoved by our screams and tears.

Welts were everywhere. In those days there was no such thing as child abuse. There was also no such thing as long pants for boys until we were thirteen or fourteen years old. After such a whipping, the scars and bruises were so visible, when your friends saw them, and eventually they would, they'd laugh and tease you for a while.

That evening, with five-year-old Odessa and two-year-old Fred napping, Mama went to her usual prayer meeting at the church. Lloyd and I finally recovered from the whipping; so, we went out front and played basketball with a couple of boys in the neighborhood. The basket was made from a wooden half-bushel basket with the bottom knocked out and nailed to a light pole. Just as we were getting into the game, Daddy came home. He walked right by us and into the house without a spoken word. We played until he called us in. He was eating a bowl of the beans and a piece of possum. He had the possum's head in his hand and was opening and closing the mouth, teasing little Fred, who had awakened from his nap, gazing as if he was witnessing magic.

"Your mother told y'all to shell those beans." Was all he spoke.

Lloyd and I stood frozen. Daddy continued to play with Fred and never said another word to us. We knew what was coming, but were too afraid to tell him that Mama had already whipped us. So we just stood there quivering. We just could not take another beating. There was no place on our lower extremities to land another stroke. It was then that I prayed my first prayer without moving my lips.

"Lord, please let Mama come home so she can tell Daddy she whipped us already. And please let her come straight home and not hang around church talking to people."

Lloyd may have been praying too, but we both remained silent, standing side by side. Daddy took his last bite of food and pushed himself from the table, when Mama walked in looking like an angel.

"What's going on?" she asked, noticing us standing like terrified statues.

"You told them to shell those beans," Daddy answered.

"I whipped them enough, Jody. Look at them legs."

Daddy never looked at our legs, didn't say another word, and never beat us. I realized then that the good Lord does hear and answer prayer.

CHURCH IN THE COUNTRY

Attending church in Windsor was always special. We only went once a summer, preferably in August. Because of the two-mile or so distance, the children had to walk barefoot almost the entire way. We would leave from Grandma Joyner's house and walk out the back and across the property of a couple of farms, across the main highway and railroad tracks. Just beyond the tracks was a deep wooded area that we'd walk through for about 100 yards, then another mile through an open field until we reached one of our relative's homes, about a quarter of a mile from the church. We'd rest there just long enough to put our socks and shoes on, and then walk the rest of the way to church. Our feet were cramped and uncomfortable in our shoes, but we didn't care. We had fun just being together, the adults chatting along the way, paying little attention to us young ones picking up sticks, bugs, and anything else we could find and play with.

The singing, preaching, and fanning, the good ole country ham, fried chicken, potato salad, greens, cake, and homemade ice cream made it all worthwhile. Then we'd walk back to our relative's house, take our shoes and socks off again, and begin the long trek home to Grandma Joyner's house.

I began noticing something after church. When we got home and changed our clothes, Mama and her three sisters – Doris, Margie, and Gladys – would sit around that old scratched mahogany table and gossip about everything and everybody in the church.

I remember one Sunday going to the same church as I had while staying with Grandma Joyner. The church was approximately twelve miles from Aunt Izona and Uncle Kenneth's house. We traveled by horse and wagon. Two horses were hooked onto the wagon, and my aunt and uncle sat on the front bench together as Uncle Kenneth guided the horse. The rest of us either sat on the floor or on a little stool or bench. We had to leave home around seven o'clock in the morning to arrive at the church by eleven o'clock. We didn't mind the extra-long day because of all the food and fun we'd have after the service. However, in that aunt and uncle's house we did not hear any gossip after church.

Hog killing time was also entertaining. Normally, killing them was somewhat of a community affair, generally done in the cold weather to prevent the meat from spoiling, and so that it could be cured by the time the weather was warm. Whenever we visited the country in the summer, Mama would negotiate for a piece of cured meat. One piece of pork in our house would last a couple of months because it was considered a delicacy. There was no such thing as a refrigerator or freezer. All we had was an ice box with two compartments. The top held the ice, which was delivered once a week. The food was stored in the lower compartment, and the air from the ice above would flow down and cool the food below.

Almost everyone in the country had a smokehouse, which was well insulated with thick wood, and a stove that provided the smoke to cure the meat. The method I saw my family use for killing hogs was to kill at least two of them on the same day. Two people would turn the hog over on its back, while the third person would use a sharp butcher knife to thrust into the throat and slice down to the heart. After the hog died, it was submerged into a long trough of hot water close to boiling temperature. Afterward, we children would use corn husks to scrape off its hair. The hog would then be hung up for carving.

It was amazing to watch my uncles cut the hog so skillfully, splitting the hog down the middle and removing the insides, including the chitterlings, liver, kidneys, and brain. The women would clean the organs and fry everything but the chitterlings, which would be slow-cooked along with the feet. The ribs would be roasted and the ham shoulder and head smoked for a future meal. We would joke that the only thing we couldn't eat was the "grunt."

It became a New Year's Day tradition that a man be the first person to enter someone's house after midnight in order for the family to have good luck the rest of the year. So we would cook part of the hog's head, preferably the jowls, divide it up, and deliver them to different families. Then we would enjoy our own with black-eyed peas and stewed tomatoes.

FUN AND GAMES

In 1936, when I was ten and Lloyd was thirteen years old, we moved to a larger house just in time to welcome our new baby sister, Rosa Jane. This house had a basement, where Lloyd and I frequently boxed. Coal was stored in the back of the basement for cooking and heating the house. Many times I would open the little window down there for ventilation and slide on the coal to the basement floor. I would end up being the blackest child in the neighborhood.

This house also had plenty of land – a little more than a quarter acre – where we played softball, football, croquet, and pitched horseshoes. Most importantly, along with the chickens, we were able to raise a couple of pigs, guineas, ducks, and even a cow, which provided us with meat, milk, and eggs. Mama and Daddy planted a garden, and we would pick our own huckleberries, blackberries, and dandelions with which Mama made gallons of wine. She never drank any, but Daddy and his friends did. They would all gather in the living room or out in the yard with their brew, and Daddy would entertain with his fine guitar playing.

We were always amazed at our father's self-taught ability to play the guitar, which was his favorite pastime. He couldn't read music, but his ear was sharp enough to give him perfect pitch and an extraordinary talent for playing a song after only hearing it once or twice. He could remove those guitar strings, replace them with new ones, and tune them by ear. The strings would be in perfect tune with the piano strings without him ever having to touch a key in the process. I don't ever remember a time in my life when he didn't have his guitar nearby.

Sometimes Daddy would find pieces of wood throughout the yard and, with the jackknife he kept stored in his pocket, would whittle harmonicas or flutes. Many of those handmade instruments ended up in the hands of neighborhood kids. Then we'd have fun making up songs as best we could, dancing and playing musical chairs. When Daddy entertained his friends, we always had fun. If they didn't know the words to songs he played, which they rarely did, they would create their own. Lloyd and I could sometimes get their attention by dancing or singing along. Our voices weren't as skilled as Daddy's guitar playing, but we could at least sing in tune, or so we thought.

Growing up during the Great Depression forced us to learn to improvise. During the warm months, we'd play baseball if we could afford a bat and ball. Otherwise, the main game was shooting marbles on our knees. Most boys wore short pants that came just below the knee. So, if the pants tore or wore out from playing ball or other games, they would have to be repaired, which usually meant stitching a patch that sometimes didn't match the pants at all. That led to jokes like, "too poor to buy another pair." Of course, most of us were too poor to buy much, so no one who was the butt of the jokes cared much.

It was a blessing if you could find a skate, take it apart, nail one part to the front of a board, the other part to the board's back, and glide around the neighborhood. Today we call it skateboarding. We would also have a lot of fun using a bicycle wheel to race each other. We would strip the spokes out of the wheel, bend one end of a wire clothes hanger to curve and fit under it; then, bend the other end to hold and push it, guiding it as we raced. The object was to see who would get the farthest the quickest without losing control of the wheel.

When our elementary school was built in 1930, there were separate boys and girls bathrooms outside. They were adjacent to one another, and we used them as a backstop for the catcher when we played baseball. The boys also played horseshoes and soccer when shoes and a soccer ball were available. Even in poverty, we adjusted and enjoyed our lives.

One summer, Lloyd and I were staying in Virginia with Grandma Joyner. We had worked a long day chopping grass from around the peanuts, when something hilarious happened. After dark, we did our usual slingshot shooting at the bats that frequently flew near the house. At bedtime, we boys slept on the attic floor, on a paper-thin mattress called a pallet. I was about nine at the time, and I bunked with my cousin, Russell, who was about six months younger than I. Two older uncles, June and Hyde, slept a couple of feet away on an 8"-high cot. If I stood up and stretched my arms, I could almost touch the boards on which the roof was nailed. Lloyd slept on another pallet with Alonzo, our youngest uncle, who was a year older than I.

I don't remember the attic floor ever being swept or scrubbed the entire summer we were there; therefore, the chinches (also called beg bugs) waited in the cracks in the floor until the lights went out. Then they would appear like little vampires searching for blood meals. Their diet was human blood, and every time we felt that pinching bite, which was constant, we'd have to smack them off of us. This was almost a nightly ritual, disrupting our rest. Every now and then we would pour a little turpentine in the cracks for temporary relief. During the Great Depression, though, you could hardly afford to buy another bottle of anything.

Those chinches were protected under solid backs, making it difficult to crush them with our fingers, but when we did, blood would spew out. Russell and I had been bitten so many times that one night, we thought it would be a good idea to light matches and burn as many as we could before they ventured out of the floor seams. Russell torched bugs on one side and I on the other. We were really burning them good until we got tired and drifted off to sleep. Before we knew it, we were awakened by Aunt Doris hollering, "Fire! Fire!"

The mattress was smoldering ever so slowly on Russell's side. We were so tired, we didn't smell a thing. Aunt Doris ran up to the attic, grabbed the pallet out from under us, and threw it out the attic window. The next day, we wrote a little song about the experience:

> *Sittin' on de corner, doing a bit of harm*
> *Yon come de sheriff and took me by de arm*
> *Took me 'round the corner, rang a little bell*
> *Yon come de buggy and took me straight to jail.*
> *Woke up Monday mornin', looked up on de wall*
> *De chinches and de bed bugs, playin' a game of ball*
> *De score was six to none, de bed bugs were ahead,*
> *De chinches knocked a home run and knocked me out de bed.*

We would just sing and laugh. We were so poor, we laughed about anything.

INTRODUCTION TO EDUCATION

Like most parents during the post-World War I era, mine considered education a must, even though my mother, Lillie, had only completed the fourth grade. As the second oldest child of eleven siblings, and the oldest girl, Mama had to assist with the younger ones, as well as work on the farm.

Daddy, the oldest in his family, left school after the third grade to work on his family's farm, as well. During the short period of time they were in school, however, they excelled. Daddy even remembered a word he spelled in class to win a spelling bee, "KABIBONOKKA." I saw this word in a dictionary once when I was young, but I've not seen it since. On Sundays, Mama and Daddy would spend half the day after church reading the newspaper headlines. I can vividly remember that Lloyd and I would sometimes lie on the floor and read whatever we could get our hands on.

My elementary school went from the first to the seventh grade. There was no such thing as kindergarten. I was able to begin first grade at five and a half years old. Back then, the deadline for starting school at five years of age was the last day of February, and my birthday is February 15. I was, therefore, frequently the youngest in my class. I enjoyed walking the six blocks with Lloyd and the other neighborhood children to the red brick single-story schoolhouse. The classrooms were quite small, almost quaint.

We had five teachers, including the principal. One teacher, Miss Howard, taught first and second grades. Miss Queen taught third grade and Miss Mary taught fourth. The fifth and sixth grades were taught by Miss Lee. Dr. Pinkney, the principal, taught the seventh grade. They all lived in Baltimore City, roughly twelve miles away, and Dr. Pinkney would transport the other four teachers to our little school. They arrived promptly at seven thirty in the morning and did not leave until every student had left the school grounds.

Dr. Pinkney was some teacher, one of the best I've ever had anywhere. He would teach math all morning and afternoon, allowing each student to use the blackboard to work out his or her math equations until he was confident that everyone understood the mathematical process. The same was true with English and history. His teaching of reading and storytelling, either biblical or novelistic, was done in such a vivid manner that would keep the whole class spellbound. He always emphasized that math, geography, history, and English were the most important subjects.

My parents stressed that teachers were to receive the utmost respect. One day, I believe I was in second grade, my parents heard something about my misbehaving in school. I had never heard my parents argue nor raise their voices at each other or us. They never talked negatively about other adults around us. When I came home from school that evening, instead of the usual warm and pleasant greeting, it seemed as if I was at a funeral. The look in their eyes was frightening. After some silent moments, they said, "We heard from your teacher today."

They chastised me just a little and emphasized repeatedly the importance of an education. From that day forward, when I came home from school, I went directly to the dining room table and completed my homework without taking off my coat or doing anything else. Because of that early experience, I came to realize the virtue of studying before a lecture on any given subject. It was a lesson of discipline and preparation that assisted me in most of my future academics.

With my rudimental experience in that tiny brick schoolhouse complete, and my academic discipline intact, I travelled by streetcar over thirteen miles north to Dunbar High School to continue my secondary education. Dunbar High was connected to Dunbar Elementary in a very densely populated section on the east side of Baltimore City. The classrooms were crowded because it was the only school on that side of town available to black students.

Since I lived in the far southern part of Baltimore County, the fare was an extra nickel once we crossed the county line into the city. Therefore, every day I would walk the rest of the way just to save that nickel. Not only that, my main lunch consisted of a biscuit with watermelon rind preserves or some other preserve my mother would make. A bowl of soup was a nickel, and a half pint of milk was three cents, which was an extra treat. I was teased almost daily in the cafeteria; so, the cooks were kind enough to have a nice lunch prepared for me a few times during the school year.

Three of us from Turners Station Elementary School entered Dunbar together. Howard Flournoy, Inell Hill, and I had been together since the first grade and were the best of friends. There were more than forty of us in the homeroom class that first day. Most of the city students had been together since the first grade, as well. We were the strangers, and we were scared. When the homeroom teacher called attendance, everyone had to state his or her correct address. When the three of us said where we were from, everyone started grinning and calling us "country." From homeroom, we were sent down the hall to our first class.

The first class of the day was history. Ms. Lottie Chase was a 5' tall, loud mouthed, no-nonsense teacher.

"No talking or misbehaving in my class," she boomed. "We work in this room!"

Everyone tip-toed to Ms. Chase's class and sat quietly, knowing better than to speak above a whisper. She called the roll quickly and stood up to begin the lesson. The first question she asked was about the Revolutionary War. It was a coincidence that one of my favorite experiences in elementary school was learning about that particular war.

"When and where was the first battle of the Revolutionary War fought?" she demanded.

After a long few seconds of silence, I blurted out the answer without raising my hand. "The Battle of Lexington and Concord."

"When and what battle was the last?" she asked, more gently.

"Yorktown, 1781." I answered again before she could call on anyone.

She focused more in my direction as she asked her final question, "When and what battle was the turning point of the war?"

"Battle of Saratoga, 1777." Howard blurted out before I could.

"Where do you all come from?" she asked.

"Turners Station." We answered simultaneously.

"Well, give me Turners for history."

The students said it was the first time they had ever seen Ms. Chase excited. She rearranged the seating and made me sit in the center on one side of the room and Howard in the middle on the other side. The rest of the classmates sat around us for advice. That sealed our fate – we were the class heroes.

Ms. Chase gave me a score of 95 the first quarter and 98 the second quarter. I didn't know what grade Howard received, although he seemed satisfied. I received similar grades in math. Math wasn't a great experience for me because I was much more advanced than the rest of the class. The teacher couldn't teach me anything for two years. I just sat in the rear of the class and listened out of respect, or worked on other subjects, particularly Latin. Sometimes I would whisper answers to the fellows sitting back there with me, which helped me become even more popular.

DISCRIMINATION FROM A BLACK TEACHER

By the time the second semester rolled around I had made a few more friends. I bet one of them that if I made all "A's," he would have to give me a nickel, to which he agreed. Money was so tight because of the Great Depression, a nickel was almost worth ten dollars today. So I studied hard and did my homework on time. I was doing well, except in one subject – history.

My new history class was held in a portable room outside the main building. As I recall, the teacher was very short and dark, with rotten teeth. She immediately assigned me to the first seat in the middle row. She always taught class with her back toward me. I studied hard and knew most of the answers, but she never called on me or even acknowledged me. Most of the class was aware of her hostility. I learned early on that an adult may say the right things, but their body language, or kinetics, reveals their true emotions. Also, discrimination is not based solely on race.

I ended up receiving a grade of 85 for the first marking quarter. I studied even harder during the second quarter. I even stayed after school and studied with a few others. She still refused to acknowledge me; so, I didn't participate in any class discussions. I received another 85 or "B" for the second marking period, while a few others who knew less than I received higher grades.

I assumed then that teachers often met and exchanged opinions about certain students, imparting their own conclusion about the caliber of the student. I never said a word, and I felt it would be futile to complain to my parents because they probably wouldn't have had the time to address it, living so far away. They were pleased that I was doing generally well. But, I knew she was not being fair. Dr. Pinkney, my seventh grade teacher, made it a ritual of openly praising a student for anything he considered worthy of a compliment. I admired all the teachers I have had, black and white, except that one, and one other.

Many years later, when I was studying at Drew University for my doctor of ministry degree, some classmates informed me how obvious it was that one professor seemed to resent me after I turned in my first paper. He rarely looked me in the eye and was very critical of any contributions I made to the class. I suddenly became ill during that semester and had to have an emergency quadruple bypass. This caused me to miss the remainder of the class. God blessed me because, not only did I fully recover, but when I repeated the class the following semester, I was assigned a different professor. This professor influenced my learning experience in such a positive way that, years later, I was happy to have him come to the church I was pastoring to teach members and clergy in the community an *Introduction to the Steps of Pastoral Counseling* class.

During the summer before my senior year at Dunbar High School in 1942, some of us students were selected to attend Douglas High to take accelerated courses so that we could graduate in February 1943, instead of June.

At the beginning of the second semester of my senior year there was an announcement.

"All twelfth graders go to the assembly hall."

One of my teachers announced that they were going to conduct class elections for president, vice-president, and secretary.

"Nominations for president, please."

One of my classmates shot up. "I nominate Milton Holmes," she said.

I stood up and nominated Margaret Johnson.

"Any other nominations?"

No one spoke.

"The nominations are now closed. All in favor of Milton Holmes please stand."

Everyone in the class stood up but me. I had no idea this country boy had gained the respect of my more sophisticated city-dwelling students.

"All in favor of Margaret Johnson please stand."

I was the only one in the room who stood up. The elections closed and I became the senior class president, graduating from Dunbar High in February 1943, one week before my seventeenth birthday.

I knew my mother couldn't attend my graduation because we lived thirteen miles from the school, and the only transportation available was by streetcar. She also had four younger children at home: Odessa, thirteen; Fred, eleven; five-year-old Rosa Jane; and three-year-old Delmus. Since the effects of the Depression were still being experienced, Daddy worked the evening shift, which also prevented him from attending. Although Aunt Margie and Uncle Jess Butler, along with Aunt Doris, lived two blocks from

63

the school, they didn't come either. It didn't bother me, though, because I had become quite independent. I still loved them; I just figured then that since none of them had ever graduated from high school, just surviving in the world consumed most of their time.

As president of the class, I received three awards during the ceremonies – a medal for the highest grade in English, a medal for leadership, and a $200 college scholarship.

MY GREATEST LOSS

Lloyd was addicted to sports and was considered to be one of the best athletes for his age in Turners Station. Although short in stature, he was very popular. He quickly excelled in everything, including softball, football, track, soccer, and boxing. His nickname was "Homer Holmes" because he hit so many home runs.

Three years older than I, yet almost the same height, we really loved each other. We never had a cross word between us, and I admired him. We always slept together and talked. He was the best athlete and a good student, while I was the best student and an average athlete, even though I could compete with most my age.

There was a nice family of two brothers and three sisters who lived two doors from us. The older brother, Ellwood, was the same age as Lloyd. The younger brother was my age and one of my good friends. We never argued and always played well together. The older brother, however, for some reason, frequently picked on me. Every time he hit me, he and Lloyd would fight. Although Lloyd was shorter and weighed less, his hands were faster and more skilled, and he would always win.

One day, Ellwood jumped me in front of our house. Naturally, he and Lloyd started fighting. He was heavier than Lloyd and happened to back him up a little, causing him to trip over a small log on the side of the road. Lloyd fell back and Ellwood jumped on him, hitting my brother. His weight and position prevented Lloyd from getting up to protect himself. I got angry and decided to make a move on my own.

I remembered that Daddy kept a hatchet in the kitchen between the stove and the wall leading out to the backyard. This hatchet was used for killing some of the chickens we raised. I ran in that back door, grabbed the hatchet, ran back out and tapped Ellwood on the back with the blade.

"Get off him," I warned in a huff.

When Ellwood got a good look at the hatchet and the smoke steaming from my eyes, he pulled away to get up. Lloyd took advantage of the opportunity and jumped up, landing some solid punches on poor Ellwood. I don't remember them ever fighting again.

I used to look forward to following Lloyd when he played ball, which was quite often. This particular time I went with him to a ball field right in the middle of the community to watch him play a game of softball. Mama and Daddy had charged him with the task of keeping an eye on me while he played, which usually wasn't a problem because I enjoyed watching him. This time, however, while sitting with my little friends, I noticed the brother of a cute little brown-skinned girl with pigtails from school with whom I was smitten. Since he and I were especially good friends, I decided, without mentioning it to Lloyd, to walk home with him, hoping to get a good look at her. Lloyd wasn't paying me any mind anyway; he was engrossed in his game.

When we arrived at my friend's home, the cute little girl opened the door and smiled; then disappeared into another room. Forgetting about the time, I waited about two hours, even after dark, anxious just to get another look. I played with her brother for a while, glancing every now and then at the room she had gone into, hoping she would reappear. Finally, I came out of my trance and, realizing I probably would not see her again, made my way home.

My parents were boiling mad when I walked in the door and asked where I'd been. Lloyd was standing in front of them scared and stiff as a board, but never made a sound. After I mumbled about my whereabouts, Daddy ordered us upstairs. He quickly followed and beat us both, saying in the midst of our cries that I should have come home earlier, and that Lloyd should have been watching me. Even at that young age, I didn't think my brother should have been beaten. Neither did he, because after Daddy left, he said, "You know Daddy whipped you the hardest." That was the last whipping we ever got.

That summer we went to Virginia for a few days, as was our annual tradition. We took our boxing gloves with us. Lloyd loved boxing and would box anyone, even those older and larger than he. And he was good enough to beat them all.

I enticed our youngest uncle, Alonzo, to box Lloyd. Although he was two years younger than Lloyd, he was still about twenty-five pounds heavier. Lloyd knocked him down with two punches.

The next oldest uncle was Hyde, two years older than Lloyd, and heavier than Alonzo. About five punches later, Hyde was on the ground. The third uncle was Junius, who was four years older than Lloyd, still heavier than Hyde, and a little faster than the rest of them. After about two minutes, he'd had enough and just quit.

In my eyes, Lloyd possessed the physical prowess of Samson or Hercules; yet, within a matter of months, we noticed that he tired easily and was aggravated with a persistent cough. One time, at a baseball game, after hitting a home run, he ran around the bases unusually slow and could barely make it to home plate. Had it not been a home run, he would have been out at second or third base. Throughout that summer, he became increasingly lethargic, yet played soccer that fall as a ninth grader, and immediately became a star. The signs were clear, though. He needed a checkup.

Mama and Daddy took Lloyd to the best black doctor in Baltimore in those days, Dr. Ralph Young. They met at Johns Hopkins Hospital where, then, no black doctor, nurse, or nonprofessional employee could work. Blacks could only be examined in the basement before admission. Then, if admitted, they were assigned to segregated wards.

Dr. Young examined Lloyd thoroughly and administered several tests. After a few days of waiting and watching my brother get progressively worse, we returned to the hospital and received the devastating diagnosis. Lloyd had tuberculosis and would have to be admitted immediately to Henryton Sanitarium, a hospital exclusively for blacks who were infected with this highly contagious disease. He would be quarantined there. Tuberculosis affected and damaged the lungs, and there was no medication available. The survival rate was poor, because there was no cure unless diagnosed early. It was a greatly feared disease in those days, and families who had infected members were often ostracized, humiliated, and even called "TB," not only by other children, but by adults as well. Our family was no exception.

Johns Hopkins Hospital was located about twelve miles from our home. At eleven years old, having only been to the hospital once, I had to travel there alone twice on the streetcar to be tested and x-rayed for TB. I was scared because I could see how sick

Lloyd was, and I had to search my way through unfamiliar territory to find out if there was a chance I could become that ill.

As soon as we found out that my tests were negative, a social worker visited us and gave us instructions on how to keep the rest of us from infection.

Lloyd was taken to Henryton, located in a wooded solitary area northwest of Baltimore, more than forty miles from home. Supposedly, the emphasis was on providing its patients with plenty of fresh air. He lived on the screened-in porch during the summer, but his only exposure to fresh air and sunlight after the season had passed, was through a couple of small window screens. My parents could visit just once a week, not only because of the distance - but now, in addition to Odessa, Fred, Rose Jane, and me - they had another young baby, Delmus Ann, to care for. Furthermore, they didn't have much money. It was still the Depression era, and now there was speculation of war. So they had to save almost every dime they earned to make these long trips to visit their oldest son. Lloyd spent most of the time there alone, with no visitors, no cards or letters, no hugs or laughter. It was as though he was confined to a leprosy colony.

Twice, Lloyd was allowed to come home for a weekend visit. By his last visit, he had had a growth spurt, shooting up to almost 6' tall, which only revealed more vividly how paper-thin he was.

After I turned twelve, the required minimum age to visit patients at Henryton, I would visit Lloyd on my own and stay until the doctors told me I had to leave. Later, the minimum age for visitation was raised to fourteen. Nevertheless, at thirteen, I would visit him repeatedly until they made me leave. I wanted to spend as much time with him as I possibly could. We would talk some, but mostly he would just lie there, barely able to sit up. He spent more time coughing than breathing.

The doctors eventually decided to operate on Lloyd and remove a couple of ribs from one side of his body, but it did little good, and his condition only worsened. I instinctively knew he would not survive. In October 1939, they wrote my parents and told them they wanted to remove more ribs from his other side. Daddy said it was no use and refused to sign a consent form, but my mother did.

In those days, very few people in Turners Station owned a telephone. It was my duty, which I liked, to go to the post office and request the mail from our box number 72. On one particular day, I ran to the post office, picked up our mail and sprinted home, knowing there was a letter from Henryton. I gave it to my mother and waited for her to read it. My beloved brother, the doctors wrote, had passed away. He had been in that sanitarium for more than two years and died on January 15, 1940. I was almost fourteen years old. I was devastated.

The next time I saw Lloyd was in our living room lying in a casket, dressed in a dark suit. Since there weren't any funeral parlors for blacks, the deceased had to be placed in the family home until the date of the burial. Sometimes I could hear my mother cry softly; yet she and Daddy remained strong for the rest of their children. When I reflect on the period, I am grieved by the fact that he had to linger for so long by himself, with none of us near to hold or comfort him.

To add to our devastation, my younger sister, Odessa, was subsequently diagnosed with an early stage of TB. This was just a few short years since her recovery from erysipelas (bacterial skin infection). She was also committed to Henryton and remained there for almost a year. She was ten years old at the time, and we feared for her life. Yet, regardless of our pain and grief, there was no grief counseling, support groups, or psychiatrist to help remove any sense of guilt, anger, or depression from the family.

In that small community in which everyone knew everyone, we were really ostracized as a family. The ravages and consequences of this incurable and contagious disease were grave, and people had a right to be somewhat fearful.

Fortunately, a woman in the neighborhood still liked my family and solicited me to sell the Afro-American newspaper, which put a few pennies in my pocket. When I wasn't selling, I was like a sponge, absorbing every word I read in those newspapers, giving me insight into the world beyond my cooped-up community. I kept myself abreast of the issues surrounding the Depression, the impending world war, and the likes of Hitler and Mussolini. I also gained respect at school because I was considered one of the smartest in my class. Learning helped fill the emptiness in a part of my soul that had belonged to my brother.

Lloyd had been my protector and confidante. I loved and adored him. He was so calm and easygoing. We never argued and were rarely separated. There are not many days that go by that I have not thought of him and really missed him.

I don't know about others, but to me, losing an older sibling and best friend at such a young age is an extremely difficult and unforgettable experience.

HOWARD UNIVERSITY

I finally arrived at Howard University and realized that I needed to get a job to be able to stay there. I met a student who was the son of one of my teachers at Dunbar High School. He recommended me for a job at the Young Women's Christian Association (YWCA). The dormitory I lived in was closer to a restaurant than the school cafeteria; so, I ate there. One morning a man put a nickel in the jukebox, as it was called in those days, and played "Boogie Woogie," by Tommy Dorsey. Before then, all I heard were the blues. It was the first song I had heard with that kind of beat.

This customer played that "Boogie Woogie" about three times, each time exciting me more than the last. I didn't want to be too obvious, but the next day I went to the restaurant early, put my few nickels in the jukebox and played the song until my money was gone. I was hooked. That evening I walked downtown to a music store and bought the record, remembering that Aunt Margie and Uncle Jessie in Baltimore had a record player. The next Saturday I caught the train there and went straight to their house. I played that record until it was almost worn out, while memorizing the melody and all the musical modulations.

A few years earlier, our church had gotten rid of its old piano and, at my parents' request, dropped it off at our house. Daddy showed me the three basic keys he knew, which every so often I played around with. I had never mastered playing the piano, but I was determined that one day I would learn "Boogie Woogie," and play it for my family.

Howard held a freshman initiation tradition where some of the upperclassmen would grab most of the freshmen guys and shave an "H" for Howard, and a "V" for Victory on top of their heads, indicating that America was at war. One night, a couple of upperclassmen sneaked into my room and seized me as their newest target. They plopped me in a chair, and a guy pinned my arms to each side. Instead of struggling and resisting, I stirred my brain for a way out. Just as they were about to flick the razor on, I quickly offered to tutor them in math, chemistry, and English if they left me alone. Luckily, I excelled in these subjects in high school and wasn't required to take English 101 or 102. We struck up an agreement, and I was one of the few freshmen who didn't stand out in a crowd.

Throughout that entire year, working and studying consumed all of my time, which deprived me of any kind of social life. I became so exhausted and lost so much weight, I became ill. By the end of the summer session, I had to leave the university permanently.

Until then, I had never missed a day of school. I believe I rarely got ill because of my parents' prescriptions. There was this nasty, slimy castor oil that we had to take twice a year to clean us out. It did. If we started coughing, we had to take the bitter three sixes, which was a cold remedy that could be taken with or without quinine. My parents opted for the one that included quinine. We'd suck on an orange to help neutralize the burn. We were also required to keep a small 1″ bag containing that stinking asafetida pinned to our undershirts to keep germs away. It also kept everyone else away. No one wanted to sit next to us in class because of the odor. Those old remedies must have been effective though. At least, until this point, when my body had worn down to a point that made it difficult to get enough rest to recover. At home again, I slept twelve hours a day for two weeks.

EMPLOYMENT DISCRIMINATION

A load of pressure was steadily lifted as I rested and regained my strength. Now it was time to look for another job in order to save money and return to school. Overall, jobs were plentiful since the Great Depression had subsided and America had now become entrenched in WWII. Hundreds of thousands of men, including heads of households, either enlisted or were drafted, which left a huge prospect in job availability for those left behind, including women. Besides the lucrative steel industry, defense plants were sprouting up everywhere to manufacture war materials. I applied to one in my area, near Bethlehem Steel in Sparrows Point.

Rheem Manufacturing Company produced military products, such as steel barrels, water heaters, and water tanks. Whites not only worked the highest paying jobs, but also received production incentives. Blacks were given menial tasks, such as dragging metal sheets to the whites, who put them through the machines, forming them into barrels. The blacks then had to attach the tops and bottoms to them, with no incentive. My job was to paint them.

It felt as though blacks had to fight three wars at the same time; one at home, another in the military, and a third one against foreign nations. It is a no-brainer why so many of our black youth feel it is no use getting an education.

Blacks and whites were non-communicative and used separate facilities at Rheem, including restrooms and water fountains. Our lunch time was limited to our segregated locker room or outside on the platform. We could smell their hatred from a distance. It mattered little that we needed to assist each other in the war effort. They resented our presence, and small fights regularly broke out.

Regardless of the ever-present discrimination exposed at the plant, I learned quite a bit about how civilians were responding to the chaotic world around them. Women worked well for the war effort by helping to build aircrafts and performing other tasks. They did heavy duty work for half the men's pay, but they were a strong force for the country. I began to respect them more because of the type of work they did and the dedication with which they performed.

Before the war, the men worked while the women were housewives or domestics. During the war, however, with the men gone, women took over a large portion of the labor. The term "Rosie the Riveter" represented these women who worked in war plants as riveters, welders, and lifters.

Contributing to the war effort also became a real transformation for the African American woman, although there were several altercations because many white males didn't want to work with blacks. The women, black and white, set a higher standard in a time of civil segregation because they willingly worked side by side. They understood that they were working for the same cause - to aid and protect our country.

One day, after working at the plant for about two months, I became nauseated from the smell of paint. I kept gagging, trying to throw up. But sitting down or taking a random trip to the bathroom was not tolerated. So guiding the hose nozzle, I just kept on spraying. The following day, with my head spinning and my stomach still nauseous, I stayed home. My only distraction was thoughts about how I fit in within my community and on my job. Frustration was mounting because we couldn't form a neighborhood baseball or football team since most of the guys my age had been drafted or enlisted in the service. Other activities were scarce for those of us in Turners Station, and I wanted to leave Rheem and home for good. I wanted to go where I could continue to learn and establish some type of discipline, even in the face of discrimination.

The following day I was well enough to return to work. When I arrived, I discovered the whites had thrown several rolls of toilet paper in our locker room and had knocked one of our guys in the head with a wrench. I told my father that evening that I wished I had been there because I would have organized our guys to fight back.

"You will go to jail for hitting one of them, but they will not go to jail for killing you," he advised.

Fortunately, within a week or so, my illness returned even more severely, and my father warned me that the paint fumes would one day kill me. I took his advice and resigned. Except for bus fare to work, I had saved all the money I made. With most of those savings I bought my first automobile, a 1936 black Buick Century, with fender wells in the front fenders storing my two spare tires. I paid $300 cash for that car.

In 1943, an automatic transmission was not available. Cars had only a gear shift and a clutch, which meant there were four movements to get the car to its proper driving pace. The idea was to get the car in third gear to save fuel and maximize the speed of the vehicle. Therefore, the car was started in neutral and then shifted to first gear at the lower left, then the shift was moved upper right to second gear, and down to the lower right to third gear, moving in the shape of the letter "H." The fourth gear, which was reverse, was the upper left. If you tried to drive beginning in third gear, the car would cut off because there was too much strain on the motor. The gear shift was moved from one gear to another by releasing the right foot from the accelerator, simultaneously pressing the clutch to the floor with the left foot while shifting the gear with the right hand; then, between shifts, releasing the left foot while pressing the accelerator with the right foot. This was repeated until you ended up in third gear, now able to drive smoothly.

In those days, during WWII, there weren't many cars on the road, and only a small number of traffic lights. There was an unwritten code in Baltimore. If you happened to stop at a red light, and another car was next to you, all you had to do was position your car in the first gear and race the motor three times without moving the car. If the driver in the car beside you did the same thing, it meant you would race as soon as the light turned green.

I participated in a few races within a two-month period. Most of the time we could race about a mile before the next red light. My car was big and heavy, which meant I lost most of the races. One time, though, I pulled up beside a car on a road that we knew stretched about five miles before the next red light. The run went past Morgan State College in East Baltimore.

When we took off, I was about a half block behind during the first mile. In the second mile I crept closer, and by the third, I was near his left rear wheel. I drove beside him and passed him in the fourth mile. I had finally won a race. After that, we stopped and talked.

"Man, I thought I had you beat and you had turned off somewhere, because at a point, I couldn't see you. All of a sudden, there you were beside me, and then you left me," he said.

"I got you going downhill," I laughed.

My car was so heavy it would pick up speed on its own traveling downhill. That evening I realized to pass him, I had to have been going at least eighty-five miles per hour in the city. It dawned on me that on that narrow two-lane highway, we were lucky not to lose control.

Not long after that race, the car began losing oil, and the spark plugs would get coated with thick carbon, barely allowing me to make it the twenty-five miles home from the city. By the time I did get home, after having to stop at some red lights, the car would barely move because of the clogged plugs. My father said that in the process of changing gears and driving so slow, the plugs would become more clogged.

Route 40 was a new thoroughfare in Baltimore City, with traffic lights about every five miles. Whenever I visited or hung out in the city, I would wait until around midnight before starting home. Nobody would be on the road but me. At a certain point the road would start downhill on a slight decline. I would come to that hill, and by the time I reached the bottom, about a mile and a half later, I would be driving well over 100 miles per hour. As I continued home, the car would run smoothly until I was around two miles from home. I always said a little prayer, especially during those final miles, and God always got me home.

UNEXPECTED DETOUR
TO HAMPTON INSTITUTE

One night, Richard, a neighbor and close childhood friend, and I decided to go to a dance at Dunbar High School so I could see some of my old friends. Since he was such a mild person, I was surprised when he showed me his pistol.

I happened to see a counselor there who told me about an exam to get a free education in engineering at Hampton Institute in Virginia. To qualify, I was required to take a two-hour written test.

I readily took the exam and later received notice that I had passed and would have to report to Hampton Institute. I was excited, unaware that I was about to take an unexpected detour.

"Boy, you're in the Army now," the soldier smirked.

His eyes looked at the black trunk I held at my side as I stepped down from the smoky train. Then he gave me a swift visual once-over as if I didn't matter.

"Just put your address on that trunk and leave it on the train. It'll be delivered back to your home."

I was shocked. He had to be kidding. Almost every dime I earned during my brief stint at the Post Office throughout the Thanksgiving and Christmas holidays, a little over $100, had been spent on those clothes for college. They had been meticulously packed in a cheap pawn shop trunk that I had also bought. All I had left in my pocket when I arrived in Virginia was $5.00.

I was so dedicated in my position in the Post Office that my supervisor complimented my work ethic and encouraged me to stay permanently. Employment there had been dependable, especially during the Great Depression and the war. But I wasn't interested. I wanted to go back to school and study my way to a more professional position. Not to mention the fact that I truly respected and enjoyed the learning process.

The soldier spun a 90° pivot and marched toward the lone military jeep outside the station. I stepped along behind him, convinced this was all a bad joke. After all, my purpose for attending Hampton Institute was to further my education, not to join the army. Humiliation and fear gripped me for a few seconds, but I had long learned to control those emotions.

I was also disappointed when I realized that I could not wear the clothes I had spent my meager earnings on, not here on Hampton's campus, not as long as I was in the military. At seventeen, I had unwittingly joined the millions of men and women who had enlisted in the military to fight for our country. And I thought I was smart.

Many colleges and universities had complained at the draft age decision because it meant a real depletion in the number of high school graduates who could enroll in their freshman classes. This would place many of the institutions in a tenuous position. In favor of appeasing them, the government incorporated some of their training programs directly on college campuses.

Eleanor Roosevelt, President Franklin D. Roosevelt's wife, was instrumental in extending the opportunity to African Americans, and Hampton was one such institution designated as an educational training ground for academically talented army cadets. I realized that the war effort afforded many of us who could not otherwise obtain a post-high school education with such an opportunity. We soldiers at Hampton were involved in this particular training.

The courses included trigonometry, chemistry, physics, history, geography, and English. There was also a strong emphasis on physical education. If successful, what typically took three to four years to achieve would be completed in eighteen months. Unfortunately, the powers that be presumed that blacks would never qualify for such a discipline. It was rumored that the minimum IQ requirement was between 115 and 120, and that there weren't many blacks who even held such a high intellectual status. At best, we would falter along the way, and prove we were truly an inferior race of people.

We proved otherwise.

The Army Specialized Training Program (ASTP) at Hampton Institute was an all-black unit of about sixty of us, with only thirteen in my class. There was another black unit of about three hundred sailors on campus simultaneously, but they were not involved in the same type of specialized academic training as we were.

I quickly immersed myself in my new life and surroundings. Besides the rigorous educational focus, pride and discipline were established, regardless of one's background. We were required to be dressed in uniform at all times and conduct ourselves with strict and unified behavior. It was constantly drilled into our heads that we were an elite unit and had to display perfect discipline on and off campus.

We marched to and from class together, we ate together, studied together, and developed a sense of camaraderie, something I had deeply missed without my older brother, Lloyd.

Our day began just after dawn with a quick shower and shave. Then we marched together to the cafeteria for breakfast. Academics were conducted from eight in the morning until four o'clock. We took one break for lunch, then we'd return to class for additional lectures and labs. After supper, we had about an hour and a half of either drilling or physical training, which consisted of group games and individual challenges. I considered myself to be a decent competitor, since I grew up near a large baseball field where the guys in my community regularly played baseball and football. I learned quickly that other predominately black communities produced some very talented athletes who were better than I. Later, there was at least two hours of compulsory study in the study hall under close supervision.

One of our outstanding performers at Hampton was Harrison Dillard, a hurdler, who was in the class ahead of me. Most days, we would see him line up several chairs to practice hurdling. We were all impressed with his ability to improvise and dedicate himself to improving his performance regardless of the lack of necessary equipment. He badly wanted to compete for the United States in the 1948 Olympics but failed to qualify in the hurdles, his specialty. He did, however, make the team in the flat dash, the 110 meter, winning the gold medal. He later won the gold medal in hurdles in the 1952 Olympics.

Dorm room lights were out at ten o'clock, with only a light in the hall next to the bathroom. I often studied in the hall late into the night. During the week there was very little socialization with other students outside the program, so much so that even attempting to get acquainted with the female students on campus proved futile because of the rigid schedule. Also, I had developed the habit while in high school of studying in advance the work that would be introduced in the next class, and I continued that ritual in college.

I did, though, have other reasons for studying as hard as I did. The rule was that if you made an average of 85 on your exams the previous week, you were permitted to go to the movies on campus on Wednesday nights. You could also leave campus on Saturdays at noon and return Sunday night before curfew. My classmates rarely made either, but I never missed either. Every Wednesday I went to the movies, and on weekends I visited my extended family in Windsor, Virginia, which was more than sixty miles from Hampton.

As long as I wore my uniform, I could ride any mode of transportation for free. I was so excited about seeing my cousins, aunts, uncles, and grandmother, I didn't mind riding a streetcar to Fort Monroe, a ferry to Virginia Beach, the bus to Norfolk, another bus to Windsor, and finally walking that last mile to the family home. I was always greeted with heartfelt love and great food. I had developed a close relationship with my Uncle Hyde and cousin Russell, and always looked forward to spending time with them. Sometimes we'd pitch horseshoes, but mostly we'd just sit around and enjoy each other or visit some of their female friends. Most of my weeks were consumed with the business of learning, so I looked forward to just relaxing with my family on the weekends.

I still had Thomas Dorsey's "Boogie Woogie" song on my mind that I had heard in that restaurant near my dorm when I attended Howard University. So on one of those weekends, instead of going to Windsor first, I detoured to Newport News and bought the sheet music, even though I couldn't read the first note. I then went on and visited with my relatives.

One day, I heard some sailors, who were also stationed at Hampton, rehearsing some songs in their glee club. I waited outside the building until there was a pause in the rehearsal. Then I ran into the building and literally begged the pianist to just play a little of the song for me so I could figure out where to start to learn it myself. He politely obliged.

I stayed busy with my classes, weekend travels, and piano practice, which I started on my own. Months later, when I finally got pretty good at it and played "Boogie Woogie" for my family, they were shocked that I could play the piano even a little. After about six months, I was good enough to practice with several guys who also played their instruments by ear. We could play enough songs that people could dance to. For years I had a good time at parties with family and friends, because of our love for music.

My fingers have now become stiff, and I seem to have lost the ability to play music. It was good though, while it lasted.

Since some of us in my class came directly from civilian life, we weren't old enough to be drafted; therefore, we weren't eligible for any pay during the length of our stay. There wasn't any money coming from home for me, but other enlisted soldiers would treat us to a soda or watered-down beer on occasion. For my eighteenth birthday, my mother sent me a package with a cake and some oatmeal cookies. My friends and I annihilated that quicker than you could shoot down the enemy.

After three months of enjoying Hampton, the army decided to close most of the schools so that they could prepare for the invasion of Europe in June 1944. I was sent home on furlough to wait for orders, disappointed that my education was, again, interrupted. My goal had never been to enlist in the service, yet I had embraced the classes, my fellow cadets, and the entire military environment.

I dreaded returning home, especially since I didn't know how long I would be there. I missed my family and looked forward to seeing them, but I didn't want to engage in another love-hate relationship with the small community from which I had come. I loved the fact that everyone knew each other. Opportunities, though, were few for me, and most of my friends were still away at war. Still, I had to return home and wait it out.

THE JOURNEY TO TUSKEGEE

I arrived home on a Friday, the latter part of March 1944. My family and I were happy to see each other, and I could tell they were proud of me. My younger brother, Fred, was wearing one of the shirts I had to return from Hampton. He boasted about how he enjoyed wearing all those clothes, as if I had bought them especially for him.

Just before receiving my furlough, I received word that my friend, Richard, had gone to a community dance a few nights before and was killed while showing off his pistol again. I was deeply hurt because I knew he never started a fight. When I got home, I went to pay my respects to his family. As I stood in the living room by his casket staring at him, I realized that my teenage friend would never accomplish any of his goals and dreams. His life had ended as abruptly as Lloyd's had. My determination and ambition deepened to use education as a source to consistently improve my life and help the lives of others around me.

Just as I was settling in, visiting with family and friends, orders came for me to report to Camp Lee, Virginia, to be processed and given a physical exam. I had no idea what was before me. I just felt that when the military expressed its demands, sometimes it was without explanation. Perhaps it was the dilemma of the war effort, and we were expected to comprehend and respond without question. After the indoctrination, which took about a month, about four of us were put on a train heading west, again, without clarification. By now, it didn't bother me too much, even when we suddenly changed trains and headed south, ending up at Keesler Air Force Field in Biloxi, Mississippi.

In 1941, Biloxi officials invited the army to build a base for WWII military instruction in aviation related programs. At the end of construction, it housed a technical training center. It was there that I received my basic training.

The orientation at Keesler Field was an eye-opener. One of the things it imbued was the necessity of practicing safe sex. We were shown pictures of diseased sex organs and hermaphrodites, persons with both male and female organs. We were also informed about Pro Stations that were established in practically every city, with items to prevent one from contracting a disease. Additionally, there were United Service Organizations (USO) in every city, where ladies would meet servicemen and entertain them. Naturally, the facilities were segregated, as was practically everything else.

Discrimination in the military represented what was occurring in civilian life. President Roosevelt had issued an executive order to eliminate discrimination in the defense industries, but there was no executive order ending discrimination in the military until President Harry S. Truman took office.

At Keesler Field, blacks were assigned to a completely separate area on the base from the white soldiers. We had our own housing and Post Exchange (PX) to buy small sundries, our own mess hall, and recreational facilities. There was no Chapel or religious services for us.

When we weren't involved in basic training, we were required to cut the officers' residential lawns, work in the mess hall, or maintain the barracks and grounds, which had to be meticulously manicured regularly. And although we had white officers, they deliberately assigned uneducated black noncommissioned officers (NCOs) to train and harass us, especially those of us they considered more educated. Most of the time, those who were drilling us and assigning various minutia couldn't even read or write their names. It appeared to be a strategic move by the whites to make us feel inferior. It didn't bother me, though, because I had become an expert on the carbine and pistol, and I was used to being around others who were less qualified.

Following the five-month basic training at Keesler, I was given a ten-day furlough to return home, before reporting to Lincoln Air Force Base in Lincoln, Nebraska. I was ecstatic about escaping that punishing Mississippi heat. The ride from Biloxi, Mississippi, was quiet and pleasant at first; however, a couple of hours later when I arrived in Atlanta, Georgia, to change trains, there was an unexpected and uncomfortable turn of events.

I was the last one to board that Georgia train before heading home to Baltimore, which was about a twelve- to fourteen-hour ride. In those days, blacks were restricted to riding in the first two cars behind the engine. The only seat available to me was on the platform between the two cars. We filled up that platform quickly, and since I was the last one on, I had to sit on the floor next to the door. Of course, there was no air conditioning, and the soot blowing through the window, mingling with the hot stale air, only added to my irritation. I remained in that position the entire ride, unable to move or go to the bathroom until we reached our destination. Fortunately, by the time the streetcar had finally dropped me off in my little community, the night had settled in. My clothes and I were covered with so much soot that I was unrecognizable even as I walked past people I knew.

Years later, while working in the Post Office, I learned that blacks in some parts of the country, particularly below the Mason Dixon line, had to ride in the first two cars of a train because the soot from the engine would blow through the windows, and whites, of course, weren't to be directly exposed to it. Also, if there was an accident, those cars would suffer the most damage. It was quite different from riding on the back of a bus or streetcar, to which I was accustomed.

While I was home, Daddy drove my cousin and me to Virginia to visit our relatives. During the war, as it was throughout the Depression, the speed limit was thirty-five miles per hour, even on the highway. It was also against the law to pass a military vehicle that was part of a convoy.

I got a chance to spend time with my extended family, pitching horseshoes, playing ball, and partying at a couple of smelly smoke-filled clubs with the young women.

I drove on our return home, which went rather smoothly, until we approached a red light in Fredericksburg, Virginia, more than 100 miles from home. That's when the brakes failed. In those days, the brake lines that conducted the fluid to the brakes were made of material that was somewhat flexible and over time, would develop a hole in it. The brake fluid would leak within minutes. This was the second time the brake lines had snapped on me, but previously, I drove slowly enough on a neighborhood road to be able to drift into the woods and stop there. Luckily, this time I scraped the wheel on the curb, which allowed the car to drift along until we happened upon an auto repair shop and stopped right on the lot. It was well after midnight; so, we slept in the car until the mechanic came the next morning. He replaced the section with the hole in less than half an hour, and we were on our way. We were blessed to make it home safely.

At the end of this furlough, I was sent to my next assignment at Lincoln Air Force Base. Here, we sat idle, figuring we would be shipped out to different locations. Meanwhile, the officers there, again, decided to assign some of us menial duties like cutting the lawns and trimming the grass along the road's edge with little hand scissors, while others worked in the kitchen. I washed dishes to stay busy and to be certain I had some food. In our free time, we would play sports or go to the gym. I went to one football game between Lincoln and a team from another base, both black. A few of our noncommissioned officers played on Lincoln's team and proved to be excellent athletes, so much so that Lincoln won.

One day, I happened to see what I considered a rather attractive young lady who was also in the Army Air Corps. We ended up talking about our hometown of Baltimore. A few times, when our paths crossed, we would walk together to the gym. But every time we got together, I noticed that there was always another female soldier following somewhat close behind.

As naïve as I was, I asked Hawthorne Smith, a fellow soldier from Baltimore, what that meant. He laughed at me and said the girl I liked was owned by the one following us. Well, no one had to worry about me talking to her again. I decided to give up the pursuit of girls until I was a civilian again.

A few weeks later, Hawthorne said to me, "There's a screening test being given to learn how to fly a plane."

I was never interested in flying planes because I didn't think blacks were allowed. What was interesting, though, was that while there was no thought about flying, there was a small airfield right across the road from Turners Station, in a white community called Logan Field. We could hear the planes come and go, and sometimes my friends and I would stand and watch them, but we weren't allowed inside the airport to observe as the whites were. We knew our chances of seeing a black pilot, let alone becoming pilots ourselves, were slim to none. In fact, in those days, blacks weren't allowed to drive a streetcar, bus, or train. So it never entered my mind to even fathom flying anything as massive as an airplane. The field was later relocated from one side of the streetcar tracks to the other side in Dundalk and renamed Harbor Field. Its final move in 1950 was near Dorsey, Maryland, and named Baltimore Washington Airport. It is now known as Thurgood Marshall Baltimore Washington International Airport.

I didn't mind taking the test, since Hawthorne had decided to take it. The testing room was packed with soldiers, and we were allowed only two hours to complete it. He and I were the only two in Lincoln who passed. We were then given orders to report back to Keesler Field by the following Monday morning to take more tests and additional basic training.

That Friday, Hawthorne and I hopped a train that was supposed to take us from Lincoln, Nebraska, to Biloxi in approximately twelve hours. Since as long as we were in uniform and could travel free anywhere in the country, we gambled on a detour to Baltimore first to visit our families. He, evidently, wanted to see his girlfriend, who worked for the Afro-American newspaper, partly owned by her parents. Hawthorne had attended Morgan State College before enlisting into the service, and he also wanted to see his alma mater play football on Saturday. We were to leave Saturday evening after the game so that we could be on time for Monday morning roll call. In the meantime, we were glad to be home.

We met at the game between Morgan and Delaware State the following day. I arrived at the beginning of the third quarter, and Morgan was leading Delaware State 56-0, easily winning the game. Afterwards, Hawthorne left to report to Keesler Field on time, but Mama hadn't been feeling well the entire weekend; so, I sent a telegram requesting an extension in my travel time. The army responded that I had five days.

MY FIRST LOVE

I decided to attend my church on Sunday since I hadn't been to a worship service in almost a year. Once I entered the tiny sanctuary, I got comfortable in the back on the left side as we teenagers were accustomed. After service, I socialized a bit with a few of my friends, some of whom were also in the military and home on furlough.

There was a drugstore about two blocks from the church that sold, among other things, sheet music. I decided to take a stroll there after church to see if they sold the music to another song I had fallen in love with while stationed in Nebraska called, "Sweet and Lovely." I wanted to learn to play it on the piano. While walking, I inadvertently turned around and noticed a cute, shapely teenager about half a block behind me and, at first, didn't pay her any mind. Well, we ended up in the music section of the drugstore together. I glanced at her now and again for a few minutes, noticing her winning smile. During small talk we discovered that we were both music lovers, which made me even more interested in her. She seemed to like me, too, and after talking for a few minutes, I hesitantly asked if I could walk her home. "Sure, come on," she said.

Having been rejected by young girls for so long since Lloyd and Odessa had been stricken with tuberculosis, which hovered over my life in Turners like the plague it was, I was shocked and pleased. So, I grabbed my sheet music, and we strolled out the store laughing and talking the short distance to her house.

When we arrived, I realized I knew Louise's family very well because they had been my customers the entire time I sold the Baltimore Afro-American Newspaper. She was almost three years my junior and had rejected my smiles about two years earlier. But now, she seemed prettier and more mature, and getting to know her better was about to become a priority.

I visited her every day, which gave me the opportunity to socialize with her family, who treated me very nicely. Her father, Roosevelt, also worked at the Bethlehem Steel Mill, which we had come to call "The Point." Because he was dark-skinned, he had the dirtiest and most dangerous job from which, a few years later, he almost lost his life. One could never tell that he held such a sordid position because once he got home, he'd slip upstairs without conversation, then reappear a short time later in casual, but very neat attire. He would then become more sociable. On Sundays, he wore an attractive suit and tie, and shiny shoes the entire day.

Louise's mother remained at home, raising Louise and her three younger siblings. Mrs. Rosa Tyler and one of her sisters, Louise, were so fair they could pass for white, which allowed them the privilege of patronizing any department store where blacks were not allowed. Their children, however, weren't light enough to go inside and had to remain outside eating their treats of ice cream cones until their mothers finished shopping.

The interesting thing about Mrs. Tyler and Mrs. Lou was that their maiden name was Tyler. They married two brothers, Roosevelt and James Tyler, who were affectionately called Doody and Hack. They were equally as dark as the sisters were light. Rosa named her first baby girl, Louise, after her sister; and Lou named her daughter, Rosa, after Mrs. Tyler. Ironically, both young cousins were the oldest in their family, followed by a brother. There was also a remarkable difference between the two sisters. Mrs. Tyler, with a short stocky frame, was quiet and conservative. She was never seen wearing make-up or pants. Mrs. Lou was tall, slender, and sophisticated. In fact, she was a fine dresser, who wore bright red lipstick. She also held a job in the cafeteria at a white school.

Louise's brother, Zack, had looked vaguely familiar, but we hung in different circles, since he was four years younger than I. Louise's sisters, Geraldine and Gloria Jean, were still young children, too young for me to notice at all.

I remember one evening relaxing on the floral sofa with Louise, engaging in small talk. Her parents and siblings had just retired for the evening, after spending as much time with us as their strength would allow. Back then, most parents didn't leave young couples unattended for any length of time. Now that it was just the two of us, I maneuvered my way closer and closer to her, and just as my arm wrapped comfortably around her shoulder, a THUMP, THUMP, THUMP, pounded through the ceiling just above our heads. I jumped and cowered, while Louise sat smiling.

"What was that?" I asked nervously.

"My mother's shoe," she said. "Time for you to go."

As she led me to the door, I felt like I had just been rescued from a tornado barreling through the home. I left, though, feeling kind of smitten and anxious, with a sentimental notion that a new and lasting friendship with the Tyler family had begun.

QUALIFYING TESTS

I hopped that first train to Biloxi, Mississippi, excited. I enjoyed the ride this time because I looked forward to meeting the Red Cross, which I appreciated very much. In those days, when you arrived at a train station, there were different organizations that would walk up and down the sidewalk distributing Bibles and serving complimentary food and coffee. The Red Cross, which appeared to send mainly women on this mission, was the only group of people who would smile, look you in the eye, and wish you luck. They treated blacks the same way they treated everyone else, regardless of whether you were in the North or far South. I looked at these women differently at the time because of the role they played during the war effort. As soldiers, we looked forward to their assistance, sincere friendliness, and encouragement in the midst of hostile expressions.

Once back at Kessler, about seventy of us from various military bases who had passed the initial screening test, were separated into an isolated group to await taking additional tests to qualify for flight school. A couple of weeks later, we were given a rigorous four-day battery of written tests. As I remember, there was one long day of testing for each subject – math, English, physics/chemistry, and history/geography. On the fifth day we had a psychomotor exam to evaluate coordination, finishing with a long and thorough physical.

While waiting to see who passed, we were again isolated from the other soldiers. We could tell they looked up to us, because they knew we had taken a series of extremely difficult tests to qualify. They felt we were special, and we appreciated that.

Some of the white officers, however, eventually got together and concluded that since we were going to be there awhile, we may as well work. It hit us that while we may have been special to some, to others we were still rowing the same segregated boat.

One day, our group presented a plan to request that we work one day, and take off the next so we could play football or baseball. We were eventually allowed to do that. I volunteered for kitchen patrol, which required working twelve hours every other day, instead of eight hours. I wanted to be sure I had something to eat, because at times it seemed as though we were short of food and had to eat what I thought was horse meat. Often, when we were off duty, we played sports and cards, becoming quite friendly with each other.

Eventually, to continue the act of busyness, the officers administrated another series of basic training. That lasted about another two weeks. Suddenly, one by one, some of the guys were being shipped out, but I didn't know where.

Finally, with only a few of us left, I received orders to return to Lincoln, Nebraska. No one ever said a word, other than I was to dress in my OD's, which was a heavier cotton uniform. At that time, Mississippi was experiencing a hot and sunny March day, and we could typically wear light khakis. Since I had to travel north, I was instructed to wear a warmer uniform.

By the time I stopped in St. Louis, Missouri, it was twenty degrees, snowing and sleeting. To make matters worse, when I arrived in Lincoln at close to midnight, almost a foot of snow had all but shut down the area, as well as the air force base. No one could come to the train station and pick me up. So, I remained there in nothing but my OD's, shivering and unable to sleep.

Early the following morning, I was finally picked up and taken to one of the barracks, which was rectangular with two potbellied wood/coal burning stoves, each one apparently equidistant to each other, along the center of the floor. My bed was in a far corner, and it felt like two degrees shy of freezing. I slept in both sets of the long woolen underwear I'd packed, but with only one top sheet, a light blanket, and a heavier blanket for cover. Outside it was around ten degrees. Inside, I nearly froze.

THE GREAT WAIT

I got back to Lincoln, Nebraska, just in time for more minutia, including kitchen patrol and spurts of recreation. I wrote to Louise every day. Soldiers could mail correspondence for free, and I took advantage of the opportunity.

One evening, I attended a basketball game where I saw a guy play the "center" position in a way I had never seen or heard of before. Reece 'Goose" Tatum was drafted into the Army Air Corps and was also stationed in Lincoln. He played an outstanding game of basketball and entertained us in the process. He was a center who could hardly be stopped from scoring. With his back to the basket, he could easily make a shot using a technique he had invented, later called the "hook shot."

I played Tatum in a game of badminton one day. Regardless of where I hit that birdie, left corner, right corner, or just over the net, all he did was stretch out his long arms, barely moving any other part of his body, and slam that birdie back at me. I ran from side to side, and back and forth until I almost passed out. He sapped all my strength and beat me so badly I never played him again.

After the war, I saw him playing basketball in Baltimore. He was with the Harlem Globetrotters, a team gifted in showmanship and skill. They were exciting players with their trickery, and crowds loved them.

Two weeks into my assignment in Lincoln, I received a telegram from my mother that my father had been hospitalized. I was quickly granted a two-week furlough. As required, I stuffed everything into my duffel bag and left as fast as I could.

It was good to be home again, unwinding, relaxing, and visiting my father, who thankfully, recovered and was discharged from the hospital. I was also excited about visiting with Louise again, which I did almost every day.

Mr. and Mrs. Tyler owned an upright piano, and I would entertain them with some of my favorite songs. One was my own original version of Boogie Woogie, and the other was "Frankie and Johnny." Louise had a beautiful soprano voice, and when she sang, it lit up the room.

After a good week of enjoying my family and friends, I was notified that I had passed the exam and was to report to the Tuskegee Air Force Base.

TUSKEGEE AT LAST

I was so ecstatic that I had been selected to attend Tuskegee Institute, I cut my furlough short.

"I'm going to be with my buddies from Keesler Field," I told Daddy. "We worked hard for the opportunity, and I'm ready to go."

Since the entrance exams had been so difficult, I believed that going to Tuskegee would be an excellent opportunity to enhance my education. Those of us who had taken the exams together would be there, too, and I couldn't wait to see them. We were different; we were better trained, academically, as well as physically.

I was as excited as the rest of the cadets who had made it there when I arrived at the Tuskegee Army Air Force Base. We were but a few of thousands of young black men who had qualified to attend the school. There were only a handful of my friends from Keesler who had made it, which left me a little disappointed. The rest of the guys I had taken the tests with had failed. But I met other cadets from around the country who were ready to meet the challenges of becoming a Tuskegee Airman. I was in a class of around eighty-six cadets and was proud of myself for having qualified for the training.

Approximately four days after we had begun the first phase of pre-flight training, President Roosevelt died. It was April 12, 1945, and we were heartbroken, believing that we had lost someone who had done so much for us. I felt particularly bad because he had become our presidential leader when I was just seven, and remained in that position until the beginning of his fourth term. By then, I was nineteen.

Even though we were in a segregated outfit, President Roosevelt and his wife, Eleanor, were responsible for this experimental project, allowing blacks to pilot airplanes during the war. He was also responsible for the Works Progress Administration (WPA), and the Civilian Conservation Corps (CCC). Some of my relatives had gone into these programs during the Great Depression. Through his efforts, we were given much needed jobs. He was also instrumental in desegregating defense plants and pressuring the defense industry to provide jobs for us. However, he could not desegregate the military, though President Harry Truman managed to do that after the war was over.

By WWII, black women began to feel liberated because they were able to work in the defense plants, and at various government jobs, such as the Post Office. This opportunity eventually changed our women, as they began to demand more rights.

My high school class had studied President Roosevelt extensively. We discussed his run against Thomas E. Dewey and Wendell Willkie, and we always supported President Roosevelt. Although blacks had voted Republican since the presidency of Abraham Lincoln, now throughout America, we believed the Republicans had driven us into the Depression and Prohibition, and further segregation. Many of us, including my family, were forced to produce homemade corn liquor and wine during these difficult times, in order to have some fun and supplement our meager income.

Like all Americans, we cadets were very surprised when the president died because we had no idea how sick he was. We had the radio to hear his speeches, but we could only see his image in the newspaper and on news reels in the movie theater. We didn't have the luxury of seeing him on live television. We had never seen him in a wheelchair because it seemed always covered. Many of us didn't even know he had polio and was unable to walk. That was not a topic for discussion. When I looked at pictures of him during his tenure in office, I could tell that toward the end of the war, he was a very sick man.

Still, we learned to respect our leaders, and blacks were very loyal to him. We also felt strongly about Eleanor Roosevelt. I wasn't there at the time, but once we arrived at Tuskegee, we heard a lot about her visit and how well she treated the pilots. President and Mrs. Roosevelt were icons to us, and we were proud of them.

TRAINING BEGINS

The week following President Roosevelt's death, Class 46A began its studies on the Tuskegee Air Force Base. Instruction was conducted primarily by African American officers in charge of the program's administration, and professors who taught the academics. There were also excellent African American pilots in charge of flight training. There was only one white officer in charge of us on campus, where cadets alternated between the classroom on campus and flight training on Moton Field. We considered him to be a fair and well-qualified administrator.

Military discipline was a major objective. Mandatory responses were, "Yes, Sir," "No, Sir," and "No excuse, Sir." Calisthenics began at dawn, after which came the books. Classes included math, physics, usage of the circular slide rule necessary for flight computation, meteorology, and aircraft and naval identification. We had from three to five seconds to identify certain aircraft and ships, whether from Germany, France, Japan, Italy, etc.. If it were actual combat, we would have been able to identify enemy aircraft almost immediately, so as not to attack each other. It was reported that there were instances throughout the war, when our artillery destroyed allied planes because they could not be identified quickly enough.

Training at Tuskegee consisted of four phases of ten weeks each; pre-flight, primary, advanced, and general. The beginning of each phase was considered the lower, and the last five weeks were the upper phases. Therefore, any cadet from upper pre-flight to the general phase could give orders to the lower pre-flight, and the orders were expected to be carried out without question.

As newcomers, we were the dog-men. We could be harassed by the upperclassmen, though no one was allowed to touch anyone. The main hazing was jumping up and down, walking like a duck, and doing push-ups.

There were questions required to be answered rapidly, such as, "Do you understand?" The proper response was, "Sir, my head is made of Vermont marble and African ivory covered over a thick layer of case-hardened steel, which forms an impenetrable barrier to the ashen tissues of my poor brain." Or…

"The ostentatious and effervescent phrases just so directed and reiterated for my comprehension failed to penetrate the ashen tissues of my poor brain."

In other words, "Sir, I am very dumb and do not understand, Sir."

To me, this was fun, except when after you had fallen asleep, someone would abruptly awake you with a question that had to be answered immediately. Some of my classmates did the most complaining and protesting of the hazing. But I figured it was just a method of developing teamwork because if you were nearby one of your classmates who was being hazed, you were supposed to join in without question or being told.

One strong question was, "What is discipline?"

The reply was, "The willful obedience to the will of the leader."

Another major theme to be recited in unison was, "All for one and one for all!"

To me, it meant that teamwork and loyalty were most important. We were taught to protect each other as much as humanly possible. The motto was, "Watch his back and he'll watch yours." My father also emphasized this in teaching my siblings and me to, "Never betray your buddy."

One of the things I realized when my class entered upper pre-flight was that the new recruits in lower pre-flight had become the underdogs. The former underdogs in my class who cried and protested the loudest were now the most sadistic when they were in charge of the new cadets. Since I was second in command in upper pre-flight, I had the authority to stop the hazing from a cadet in my class.

Sometimes we would laugh at the tales the upperclassmen would tell about the flight instructors. One such story that was told repeatedly was, if the plane was going to crash, then the instructor was supposed to holler, "Bail out! The plane's going to crash!," and the trainee was supposed to jump first. Sometimes they'd say, "The instructor jumped first and then hollered back, "Jump!" They would make up humorous tales about any little thing. These kinds of stories were necessary, especially in crisis situations. Humor helps clear the mind and allows one to think as rationally as possible.

After a couple of weeks as the lowest ranking cadets in the program, there was a twenty-four-hour period called, "Dog's Day." Now, those of us in the lowest class were in charge of every class above us. If they were commanded to jump or walk like a duck, they had to obey. They had to do the same things we were required to do.

To most of us, this was a fun day. But my roommate, Cooper, was the most anxious for revenge. He harassed those upperclassmen as if he was on a suicide mission.

The special day began after supper one evening and continued through the next day. At its conclusion, practically all of the upperclassmen came looking for Mr. Cooper, as he was then called. Each room had four beds, two upper and two lower bunk beds, with at least one upperclassman in each room.

Many of the upperclassmen came to the hall near our room, waiting for a chance to get to Mr. Cooper. We had a very calm and well-focused upperclassman in our room. He just told everyone to be quiet and leave; he would take care of him. Again, the policy was that no one could touch another trainee.

All he did was tell Cooper to "pop to," which meant to come to attention, stand straight with shoulders back and knees straight. Then he had to hit the floor without his body touching it. When he fell, he was in the push-up position.

After about five hours, the upperclassman, lying on the top bunk where he slept, was still giving the order, "Hit the floor, Mr. Cooper." The next morning, Cooper could hardly bend his arms to eat or write.

Two days later, a track meet was held, and all trainees in pre-flight, primary, advanced, and general classes, who were able, were to compete against each other. Cooper and I were sitting together watching everyone warm up.

"I could win that quarter mile, but my arms and shoulders hurt too much," he said, unable to raise or extend his arms.

"Go on out there and win so you can prove you're not just Mr. Mouth," I goaded him, not really knowing what he could do.

Cooper ran onto the track without warm-ups, lined up with the other runners, and at the "bang" of the gun, ran that quarter mile with his arms at his side and beat everybody. He really gained some respect after that.

One of the most electrifying races was the 220. In our class was a cadet named Clifton Wharton. The race started with Cliff in last place. With about 100 yards to go, he had moved up to third place. As he ran, his head was swaying from side to side, as if he were gasping for air. Now, he was in second place behind the leader, looking as if he would die from lack of oxygen. I was screaming with some of the other cadets, egging him on. A cadet standing next to me whispered, "I know him. He will win."

In the last thirty yards, Wharton passed the leader so fast, everybody screamed.

Later, a boxing exhibition was held on the base. Some boxers, such as Joe Louis, the heavyweight champion of the world at that time, and other professional boxers who were considered excellent and had developed a good reputation, were invited to fight an exhibition with some of the enlistees to entertain and build morale.

One of my classmates who could fight was a cadet from Buffalo, New York, named Thomas Stenhouse. My friend, Hawthorne Smith, had told me about an exhibition at Keesler Field in Mississippi, in which Stenhouse had boxed with a professional and had held his own. Now Stenhouse was a soft spoken guy with a calm manner and a perennial smile. Although we were frequently together in our spare time, I never saw him in the gym practicing.

The outdoor stadium was packed. In the first round, Stenhouse seemed to calmly throw a few punches as if to say, "This is a fun night." But in that second round, he threw so many punches, it looked as if his opponent would be knocked out, but professional courtesy didn't allow a traveling visitor to be embarrassed. In the third round, Stenhouse eased up a little and appeared to make sure the fight was a draw.

Years later, I had read in the Sports Illustrated magazine about Thomas Stenhouse's successful boxing career. I called him at his home in Buffalo, and he told me he had become a school teacher. He boxed some after the war, but concluded that teaching was a better career for him. The learning experience he had gleaned from Tuskegee had encouraged him to pour faith and hope into the lives of our youth and community.

I was a sports fanatic in those days. I grew up either watching my brother, Lloyd, play ball, run track, and box, or competing in the same sports myself. Most weekends at Tuskegee, I played either softball or touch football. I loved them both, even though I could not consider myself the best.

Once while playing football, our team had the ball and called a running play. I went to hit a player with a cross body block, and his knee hit me in my right kidney. Naturally, it knocked the wind out of me, and I could hardly catch my breath for about thirty minutes. Then I went back into the game.

The next day we were playing softball. Although I liked to pitch, I was the catcher. Cadet Derricott, a former football star in college, was playing first base. The score was tied. A player on the other team had hit a single and was on first base. The next batter dropped a bunt down the first base line. Derricott and I ran simultaneously toward the ball with our hands down to pick it up and throw it to second. With Derricott coming down the first base line toward me, I figured he would stop because he was running away from the runner, and I was racing toward him. We met over the ball at full speed. We were both looking down at it, and that quickly, his right shoulder hit me in the right eye. Since he was heavier and faster than I, he knocked me into the air, and I landed flat on my back.

My eye began bleeding profusely, but I said, "Let's keep playing." Some of the guys picked me up by the arm and took me to the dispensary. A service man, who didn't seem like a doctor, closed the cut on my eyebrow with four stitches and fitted me with a patch. I walked around with one-eyed vision for almost two weeks.

FLIGHT INSTRUCTION

Once pre-flight training ended, we were transferred to Tuskegee Institute to begin flight instruction. One of the classes involved learning Morse Code, the main method of aerial communication at the time. The training consisted of sitting in booths around long tables. Each person had earphones, and the instructor would begin pressing his key at an increased rhythm each day. Words were spelled by dots and dits. We pronounced a period as a *Dit*, and a short line as a *Da*.

When there was danger, the signal was *Dit Dit Dit – Da Da Da*, repeatedly. The "SOS" signal meant, "Save our souls." It would be repeated over and over again, if necessary, until rescued or killed. Although I was the first in my class to be able to translate Morse Code at fourteen words per minute, others performed better than I at naval and aircraft identification. I was proud of my academic abilities there, and the ease with which I fit into the instructional protocol and disciplines of that environment.

All of us worked extremely hard to do our best, and we complemented each other by studying and sharing as a team. We often studied far into the night, until all we could do was fall asleep. None of us wanted to fail. We realized that to be undisciplined resulted in tough consequences, from the silent treatment to dismissal.

I was used to studying hard. My parents had shaped in Lloyd and me a passion for reading and exploring. Education had its benefits – a life of learning and its rewards. I studied ahead as often as possible. I was told that in my pre-flight class of eighty-six, I was in the top eight. I realized then and now that regardless of our standing, we all learned something from each other.

Aerial communication and other instruction regarding the aircraft itself, including understanding the four strokes of an engine and engine repair were at last complete. So now, we were transported to the black-only Moton Field to begin the actual flight instruction. We had observed other upperclassmen during their flight training, and wondered how we would do if we ever got the chance. Since we were at war, I figured we might die anyway; so, I may as well go ahead and fly.

Our initial instruction took place in a little PT-13, which like most trainer planes, had dual controls. The aircraft was a two-seater with an open cockpit, two wings, and propeller. Each seat was just large enough to manipulate the controls. The student sat in the front and the instructor in the back seat, their arms resting on the small of the door.

We were taught to perform several maneuvers, such as climb, roll, stall and spin while diving, similar to riding the most daring amusement park roller coaster. When coming out of the spin, you were supposed to fly in the same direction before you started the maneuver. It tested my nerves, but it was so much fun and peaceful, I didn't care. No red lights, no stop signs; just peace. I really appreciated the fact that I had earned the privilege of training to fly.

Involved in training were two support groups that the pilots could not have succeeded without. One group consisted of those who made sure the parachutes were properly assembled in case of an emergency, and someone had to bail out. I didn't take them for granted because in training, although we may have worn a different parachute each day, they all felt the same - tight and secure, and to me, could be relied upon in case of a bail out. Therefore, I felt safe.

Having bought my first big car just before entering the service, and having worked on it several times when it had lost its power, I knew that the mechanics were the other group of important personnel. I felt extremely safe because of their competence in maintaining the aircraft. When I started that PT-13, it would "purr like a kitten," as we used to say.

Learning to fly the PT-13 wasn't too complicated. The academics, however, proved to be more difficult. Graduating was equally challenging. A class could begin with sixty or more trainees, and by the time graduation came around, we were lucky if there were thirty left. We heard there was a quota to determine how many would graduate at one time.

Sometimes, the Red Tails of the 99th Pursuit Squadron would return to Tuskegee from the European theater, wake us up in the middle of the night, harass us a little, and then talk about what was going on in the war. This was a part of the first group of fliers commandeered by Benjamin Davis to engage in military tactics overseas.

The standing name for us, the pilots and the cadets, was Benjamin Davis. We all looked up to him as a leader of the Tuskegee Airmen, and as one of its first pilots. At one time, the government wanted to close Tuskegee and send Davis' first group of fighters home. But he, along with the National Association for the Advancement of Colored People (NAACP) and the Black press, fervently and steadfastly resisted their attempts, and through his efforts, we remained active. I remember as a newspaper carrier a mere four years earlier, reading about the controversy regarding the Tuskegee Airmen. The Baltimore Afro-American Newspaper strongly supported Benjamin Davis and the entire program. He was in Europe by the time I arrived at Tuskegee, but we all still had strong ties to him. We admired and respected how he had fought for the Airmen, and we did all we could to preserve the honor and integrity he stood for.

According to his biography, Officer Davis was strongly motivated by the accomplishments of his father, Benjamin O. Davis Sr., who was promoted to several positions while in the military himself; Lieutenant, Captain, Major, and Lieutenant Colonel. Officer Davis was the first African American to achieve the rank of Brigadier General.

We had many opportunities to talk with members of the 99th Pursuit Squadron. We were so proud of them and admired them for their desire to protect and defend our country, even though they weren't wanted by their own heavily segregated and discriminatory nation.

One thing that really impacted and embittered us cadets was learning that the German and Italian prisoners could eat with the white pilots, but the black pilots could neither enter the mess hall nor the club. The white pilots needed the black Airmen in order to survive the war, but we couldn't eat or socialize together. We realized that in war, there may be no color barrier in a foxhole, but the Tuskegee Airmen continued to be persecuted by segregation and discrimination.

Some nights we would sit under dim lights and discuss our future. We talked about the arrest of more than 100 Tuskegee Airmen for attempting to enter the white-only Freeman Field Officer's Club in Freeman Field, Indiana. Since it had been drilled into us that, "Discipline is the willful obedience to the will of the leader," only a few had attempted to enter the club, but many others banded together and made the sacrifice to be arrested as a group. Some were court-martialed and imprisoned. Others were given dishonorable discharges. They were pardoned almost fifty years later, long after many of them had died in disgrace and never had the chance to enjoy their vindication.

We would often debate about the issues of discrimination in the military and how we could or could not fit in. Kentucky, Illinois, Indiana, Ohio, and most other northern states were extremely hostile. Such treatment was expected in the South. We came to the conclusion that whites did not want blacks in any of their communities anywhere, even after we had fought for their security, liberty, and freedom.

I gradually became more angry and resentful, realizing that even as African American pilots in the United States Army Air Forces who had achieved academic and aerial success, we were not going to be respected in our homeland. However, the Tuskegee Airmen retained a sense of loyalty. We felt as strongly about our country as everyone else. We weren't going anywhere. We weren't going to try to relocate. This was our country and we wanted to do our part to protect it. We were willing to fight for it and die for it. But just as important, we wanted part of the pride of ownership.

I appreciated the academic experience I received with the Army Specialized Training Program at Hampton. And yet, I loved Tuskegee because there was an even stronger emphasis, not only on intense academic instruction, but also on teamwork, discipline, and honor. *All for one and one for all.* You could not betray a friend because, if you were flying, you couldn't go off on a tangent; you had to remain in formation since your buddies on either side depended on you. In terms of discipline, each was obligated to immediately obey the instructions of the leader.

Regarding honor, your word was your bond, just as binding as a signed contract. Service as a Tuskegee Airman was not about individual recognition. Neither was it singularly about academic and military excellence, which was necessary to assist in the victory of our nation. But it was also about loyalty and teamwork, which underlined what I had already learned at home from my father with his five principles. He promised that insulting an adult would never be tolerated. I realize the importance of these rules. As I get older, I see a decrease in respect and a simultaneous increase in the prison population.

A CIVILIAN AGAIN

Just as I was ready to fly solo, Japan surrendered. Some officers announced that those of us who had volunteered for the service could quit the Army Air Corps. They said, "You don't have to fly anymore, but you have to attend classes. So I went to school. We took some additional courses and played softball and football. Then we would sit up half the night expressing our bitterness at this turning point in our lives. We felt the white soldiers, especially the pilots, resented us more than any other race of people they were fighting. They protested the black pilots being stationed in their states. Considering the American Civil War, it was expected that eighty years later we would be accepted more readily than enemies from another country. But that was not to be.

Eventually, I thought if I continued in the military, I would be taking a chance. The war had ended. President Roosevelt and Hitler were dead, and Mussolini was executed by hanging. Several of us perceived that we were transitioning from WWII to yet another war, possibly requiring us to go to Japan, China, or Burma, and I didn't want to be part of it. I would have to remain in Tuskegee for at least another five or six months, committing to more time and, I predicted, possibly getting involved in another war. I wanted out.

I had been very proud of the training and exposure I had received at Tuskegee. There had never been any outbursts or exhibitions of hopelessness; just a calm, disciplined resolve that we should expect the worst and be composed enough to abide by the Serenity Prayer:

God, grant me serenity to accept the things I cannot change,

The courage to change the things I can,

And the wisdom to know the difference.

I took my orders and landed on November 8, 1945, at Andrews Air Force Base in Camp Springs, Maryland, with about five others. There we received our discharge papers. I was nineteen years old.

The eyes of the nation had been upon us. And now, my eyes were on a nation that had shunned us.

DATING

I was so excited about returning home and cementing my relationship with Louise that it didn't register until I had been home for a minute that she was still a high school student. The countless letters we had written each other rarely, if ever, mentioned her commitment to school. She was in the eleventh grade at Sparrows Point High School, a segregated school near Bethlehem Steel and Rheem Manufacturing. Then, Baltimore County schools for blacks only went to eleventh grade, which meant she would graduate at seventeen. What was exciting to her was that, as an avid poet, she had been selected to write the class song for the graduation ceremony.

Under her mother's close supervision, during the precious few hours a day I spent with her at home, I would assist her with homework and, at times, entertain her family with my growing musical repertoire.

My parents were the only members of our family who settled in Turners Station, but almost half of Mrs. Tyler's eighteen siblings and their families lived there. So, Louise had plenty of cousins near her age, and we visited with them almost every weekend. That was fun because we could have a house party at the drop of a hat.

While I was in the service, the community had doubled in size with the existence of new defense plants and job availability. There was a great migration of people from the South to work at these jobs. This required additional housing in and around Turners Station to accommodate the Black workers. Two sections were built to the west of Old Turners, as it was now called, which were Turner Homes and Sollers Homes, and two to the south, Ernest Lyons and Carver Homes. Each of these sections had a recreation center and a ball field. Some weekends, Louise and I would go to functions or activities at any of the recreation centers. At times, I would entertain guests, playing my own version of the "Boogie Woogie" and the blues on the piano, while everyone danced.

By the following spring, Louise was nearing her graduation, and the weather was warming up a bit. Mrs. Tyler had slowly begun to ease her restrictions on her, and on rare occasions, we would travel more than fifteen miles, almost two hours by streetcar to the city just to see a movie. The Royal Theater was located on the famous Pennsylvania Avenue in Baltimore City and was similar in essence to the Apollo Theater in New York City. This was the showcase for black celebrities, and sometimes we went. Also on Pennsylvania Avenue were a pawn shop, a market, other movie theaters, some night clubs, and Rice's Inn, a Chinese restaurant. It was the only restaurant I knew of in those days willing to serve blacks. Going to the Royal for entertainment, then eating at Rice's Inn, with its intimate booths and hot food, was considered a really classy date.

Daddy had given away my 1936 Buick Century while I was away in the military because no matter how hard he worked on it, it refused to run. He had also tried unsuccessfully to fix his old 1934 Chevy, and had practically given that away, too. I convinced him to help me work on it so Louise and I could drive to the city. It took almost two months, but we finally got the car up and running, with the exception of the brakes, which couldn't be repaired because they had rusted so badly. So we did what we could to make it drivable. I was able to drive for almost two years without brakes. There were never many cars around, and if I drove slowly enough to time the few lights on the road, we could travel to the city. When I thought I had to stop, I would be sure my foot was off the gas pedal, and if necessary, I'd drive close enough to the curb for two of the wheels to rub against it to stop the car. All but one of the windows were broken out, and on chilly nights, we would bring our blankets and wrap them around ourselves to stay warm.

Once Louise graduated that June, her mother told her that she had to get a job immediately. She worked the day shift and sometimes weekends at a restaurant at the then Friendship Airport. Louise had also begun taking classical voice lessons with the legendary operatic soprano, Rosa Ponselle, and her voice had grown impressively more rich and beautiful. Sometimes she would visit her Aunt Beulah in Philadelphia and attend cultural functions there, returning home each time with an increased desire to one day become a famous opera singer.

The major hindrance to Louise realizing her dream was the constancy of our relationship. It gradually overshadowed any other plans, and after she graduated from Sparrows Point High, we began to talk of marriage.

FORT HOWARD VETERANS HOSPITAL

After the war, since there was no need to produce war materials and machinery, most factories were either on strike, closed, or downsized. Ships weren't being constructed, and iron and steel were no longer necessary. Therefore, nearly everyone who had moved North for employment was out of work. The major relief for veterans was the benefits of the GI Bill, which allowed us $20 per week for a maximum of six months, or until work became available.

In February 1946, I tried to return to Rheem Manufacturing Company, the defense plant in Sparrows Point where I had worked during the war. The rule was that if you had been drafted into the military, you could reclaim your job. They informed me, however, that since I had quit and enlisted, I could not have my old job. I wasn't too upset about it, since the defense plant and I had a mutually decaying relationship anyway.

One day, I heard that the Veterans Hospital in Fort Howard, Maryland, near Sparrows Point was hiring. There I got a job as an orderly working the three to eleven shift. Most of the patients were WWI veterans, although there were a few younger WWII veterans who had contracted TB and were confined to the isolation ward. It was one of those wards to which I was assigned.

The wards were segregated, with blacks on one ward and whites on the other. The black patients were generally friendly and informal. The whites, however, were hostile and degrading. When they wanted something, some would call me "boy" or "nigger."

For a while, out of disgust, I would retaliate with some unkind words. Here they were, bedridden, needing me to bring them food, take them out of bed and sit them in a wheel chair; then periodically lift them out of the wheel chair and assist them in and out of the bath.

Yet several months later, I discovered some of those old veterans, black and white, had some interesting stories to tell. It became my style to listen to them, because they reminded me of my own story of nineteen short years. Not only had I lost my beloved brother, two young sisters, my paternal grandmother and both grandfathers, but we also battled other illnesses that were potentially deadly, including mumps, pneumonia, and diphtheria.

The veterans, young and old, brought some of my other hurts to the surface. While attending Howard University three years earlier, Mama's youngest brother, Alonzo, died at the age of eighteen. When he was about eleven, he had been struck in the eye by a splinter from the baseball bat we had made with a tree limb. Later the doctors diagnosed that the old injury had caused a latent infection and ultimately, his death. Since Alonzo, Lloyd, and I were near the same age, we had played and worked together very closely during the summers in Windsor, Virginia. Although he was my uncle, he was like a best friend to me, and I was deeply hurt by his untimely death.

Not long after Alonzo died, Uncle Hyde, who was only five years my senior, also lost an eye. During a baseball game, he hit a ball, and the makeshift bat broke into pieces. One of the pieces ricocheted into his eye. He wore a glass eye for the rest of his life. He became my favorite of all my mother's siblings. Years later, whenever I visited Virginia with Louise and our children, we stayed with him and Aunt Ethel, his wife.

Hyde was the only one of my ten uncles who served in the military during the war. He joined the Civilian Conservation Corps initiated under President Roosevelt, and was later accepted into the army. Some of my other uncles were excluded because they worked on the farms to support their families.

Although one of my maternal uncles, Leslie, was about thirty years old at the onset of WWII, he never served in the military. He was, no doubt, one of the most athletic men I knew. He could run for miles hunting rabbits, and could swim several laps at a time nonstop. He even served as a lifeguard for Edgewater Beach; yet he failed the military physical. I asked him how he beat the draft. He said he drank about a half-gallon of strong black coffee just before going for the exam. His heart was beating so fast, the doctors deemed him ineligible to serve.

My family experienced much suffering and turmoil early in my life, yet we remained strong. From these tragedies, I gradually developed a greater tolerance for all the patients at the hospital. Once I learned to listen to them, I rarely had another problem.

After about a year at Fort Howard Hospital, I received additional training and was given the title of nurse's aide, a so-called semi-professional position. Some employees were hired as janitors, while nurse's aides provided patient care.

I recall a time on the orthopedic ward when there was an emergency operation on a patient's back to fuse two vertebrae in the lower spine. This was the first time I had ever been in an operating room. After I scrubbed myself and donned a surgical gown and mask, my duties were explained to me; to make sure the light above the operating table and stools were properly positioned during surgery, then cleaning the room afterwards.

I entered the operating room just in time to see the surgeon pick up a steel hammer with one hand and bang a steel chisel he held in the other, on the patient's back. I almost fainted. I backed out the door as fast as I could, stumbled to the sink for support, and gulped as much cold water as I could without throwing up. Then I had to pull myself together in a hurry, scrub again, put on another gown and mask, and return to the operating room. This time I was determined to glance in the direction of the operation only when absolutely necessary.

I didn't think I would have that reaction because, not only had I helped kill hogs at one point, but I had also killed many chickens with that old hatchet kept behind the stove in the kitchen.

Following the surgery and recovery period, the patient was placed on my ward in a Stryker frame, which was a bed that could be quickly rotated 180 degrees so the patient could get quick relief from the pain of constantly lying on his back. Almost a month after his surgery, the men were integrated on the wards, but not the rooms. There was also a little separate section behind closed doors to accommodate about twelve white female veterans.

I gradually became accustomed to assisting in the operating room. I periodically witnessed successful surgeries, but I also saw those patients who did not survive the trauma. Then I would have the arduous task of transporting the body to the morgue. That took some getting used to.

I developed a cursory understanding of different medical procedures and recovery techniques. I also learned to appreciate and respect the doctors and their support staff for their commitment to patient care and recovery.

FIRST MARRIAGE

There were a few commitments other than our jobs that made my time with Louise extremely valuable. She was still taking voice lessons, and as the oldest, was assigned the task of doing most of the ironing, cooking, and cleaning for her family. Mrs. Tyler was meticulous and required the same from Louise.

Besides playing sports on weekends, a group of friends and I organized a men's club and called ourselves The Comrades. There were sixteen of us. One of our projects was to provide assistance to those in need. At one point, we raised enough funds to assist a family whose house had been destroyed by fire. We held dances and hosted various fund raising activities for our projects.

After almost three years of dating, Louise and I set a date to get married. On June 15, 1947, we became Mr. and Mrs. Milton Holmes. Several of my buddies in the Comrades were my groomsmen.

The following day, one of Mrs. Tyler's younger brothers, Phil, got married and arranged for us two couples to honeymoon together, which I thought was a great idea. We visited her aunt's house in Goochland, Virginia, but when we got there, Louise went into the house and started crying. She cried at least three hours the next day, three hours the following day, and every day after that for the remainder of the week we were away. She would never cry in the presence of Phil or his wife, Pearl, but when we were alone, there was little I could do to appease her. The problem was that she was never able to tell me what kept her so upset. One day it hit me that I may have married the most fragile person on the face of the earth.

Our two jobs still didn't make us much money. So Louise and I settled into her parents' cramped three-bedroom duplex. Both occupants of the semi-attached homes equally shared the same back porch and yard. A screened partition, however, separated the front porches. It was all right, though, because the occupant of the other house was Mrs. Tyler's niece, Catherine, and her husband, Horace.

Geraldine and young Jeanie had to sleep on cots in their parents' bedroom. Louise and I slept in the second smaller bedroom, and her brother, Zack, slept in the third smallest bedroom that would eventually be converted into a bathroom. While living there, I got a chance to see just how close Louise was to her mother and how strong her desire was to please her. Mrs. Tyler emitted a quiet authority, yet also wore a stroke of sadness on her face that appeared to go unnoticed. She did seem, however, to get comfort from cooking and sewing, and she was quite adept at both. Her blackberry and blueberry pies and homemade ice cream were as delicious as her fried chicken, potato salad, and chicken and dumplings. Louise spent precious time perfecting those and other recipes, not only while working alongside her mother, but also as an employee of food preparation at the airport eatery. She soon became an extraordinary cook.

The Tyler home eventually became too cramped, and like most WWII veterans, I was anxious to take on my own responsibilities. We veterans wanted to work, get married, and have a family. We often dreamed of buying a home as soon after our military discharge as possible. I didn't know what the word "apartment" meant.

After about nine months, my Aunt Margie loaned us $300 to buy a little house right there in the Turners Station community. We were the first family on both our relatives' side to have an inside bathroom and running water, particularly the bathroom shower.

I was so glad to finally be in my own home, but Louise wasn't happy at all. Although we were less than a ten-minute walk from both of our families' homes, being that far from her mother was unacceptable to her. When I left for work at three o'clock, she would walk to her mother's. Most of the time when I returned home before midnight, I could hear her crying. She would just cry and cry until close to three or four in the morning, and was frequently inconsolable. Mrs. Tyler would send for Louise's Aunt Beulah in Philadelphia to stay with us, and it worked out as long as she was there. As soon as she left, though, it was back to the same mysterious crying spells.

We decided that perhaps she would feel better if we had a baby, and she was quite excited when she found out she was pregnant. On January 24, 1949, we had a beautiful chocolate baby girl and named her Linda.

Although I had never noticed it before, I discovered soon after the baby's birth that Mrs. Tyler was very controlling. If Louise wanted to travel a mile and a half alone by streetcar to the store to buy baby clothes, her mother would discourage her by convincing her that she was incapable of buying those kinds of things on her own. So Mrs. Tyler would buy everything herself, preventing Louise from shopping alone for the baby. The only thing she could do was have Linda's bottle ready when it was time to eat.

Linda was the oldest baby and the first grandchild of both sides of the family. Every time I turned around, Daddy would be coming from one direction trying to get the baby, and Mrs. Tyler would try to beat him to our house from the other direction. There was constant conflict because everybody wanted Linda.

Less than a year later, Louise got pregnant again, and nine months later, plump, fair-skinned Janet was born. Now all of a sudden, Mrs. Tyler preferred the light-skinned baby. My parents, then, would gladly take Linda.

After Janet was born, Linda started throwing up every meal. Then she would eat a little. After this went on for some time, we took her to the hospital but were told there was nothing wrong with her. I figured that with all the attention from Louise's family centered on Janet, Linda had begun to feel dejected.

In the meantime, when Louise nursed Janet, she would have to cry for at least ten to fifteen minutes before she was fed. In those days, babies were supposed to nurse at required intervals of four hours. If they got hungry before then, they would just have to cry, but I didn't agree with this tradition. I fussed about that quite a bit, but nothing changed. At one point, we were really having a difficult time agreeing on the subject, but I knew Mrs. Tyler and her sisters were the influence behind the struggle. My parents, by now, were also involved, believing they also knew better what was best for my wife and children than I did.

Juggling marriage, babies, extended families, and now a low-paying job had become a little more complicated than I had planned.

A SURPRISED LIFE AS A POSTAL EMPLOYEE

By 1951, I had been promoted to the top level of my grade at Veterans Hospital, with an annual salary of around $1482. This was definitely not enough money to take care of a wife and two children, and pay a mortgage of $44 a month on top of that. I realized that if I stayed there, I would never be able to afford to buy another car or a larger home.

I left Veterans Hospital on Friday, November 16, 1951, and began working as a postal clerk the following Monday. This was the same place where eight years earlier I could not envision myself working. Being broke long enough, though, will make you work where you did not think you could.

I had heard the United States Post Office was hiring clerks and letter carriers, but to be considered for one of those positions, the candidate had to pass a written test to qualify, and everyone thereafter took a scheme test, which required memorizing mail routes. It meant committing to memory the location of close to 1,000 streets in Baltimore City and locating 100 of them within ten minutes or so. I easily passed the test and got the job. I bought my second car, a 1947 four-door Chevrolet, with cash I received from the annual leave I had earned from the hospital.

The first day I worked at the Post Office was a rude awakening for me. The postmaster conducted a short orientation that was to the point. You report to work on time, take your time card, stand in line, and when it was your turn, slide the card into a machine that would stamp your arrival time. We called it "punching the clock."

We were considered substitute employees or temps, with no permanent status until earning the right to be a regular, which could take about three years. We worked where we were assigned by the supervisor, and hours of work would vary from a minimum of two hours to a maximum of twelve hours a day, depending on the volume of mail. We were limited to ten hours a day, seven days a week for the first two weeks, and twelve hours a day until either Christmas or being dismissed. We were also informed about a walkway in the ceiling in which postal inspectors could enter at any time and view any employee through a one-way mirror. Most importantly, we could be fired on the spot by the supervisor without the right for appeal.

Wow, I thought, I had left a good job with low pay but good security. Now I had a better job with more money, but no security.

Discrimination was more blatant in the Post Office than at Fort Howard, and the biggest shock was displayed the following day when we reported to work. Blacks and whites stood in line together to punch the clock. Then we reported to areas where blacks were required to stand and work, while whites could sit and file mail. We were assigned to stand at so-called stacking machines and separate long business letters from the short letters in two separate slots on a moving belt. At the end of the belt was an operator who would take each letter and place it in a machine to cancel stamps for future use and apply the correct time and date on the envelopes. We also had to file flats, which were large envelopes, and process them.

Whites had the privilege of sitting on stools and filing mail in about thirty-six slots in an upright box called a case. They would only work on the stackers when the mail that was collected from the boxes in the street was heavy enough that it required another stacker to be opened. Blacks could sit and file mail after all stackers were empty.

Blacks had to pass the same scheme as whites, yet we were not considered good enough to work the same scheme we had studied. We were also not allowed to be rural letter carriers as the whites were. Rural carriers were considered political appointees and were paid extra for the use of their automobiles.

What was interesting was that in the North, blacks were required to work on the inside so as not to be seen by the public, while in the South, they couldn't work inside, but had to be separate from whites. Also in the North, blacks were the letter carriers who delivered the mail that was transported on trains.

Because I was broke, I worked ten hours every day, seven days a week for two weeks. My hours were then increased to twelve hours a day until Christmas. I was off Christmas Day but volunteered to work every day after that until Easter. During the spring and summer months, I would take off one day every two weeks. The schedule was left to the discretion of the superintendent.

I experienced quite a bit at the Post Office within a short time. Sometimes the hierarchy would place a coin in a hidden spot to see if it would be stolen. There were also times when a tray of letters would be placed in front of the worker, and a random envelope would be slit at the end with barely visible paper money. Some employees could not resist the temptation to steal the money and would then be discharged from a job that provided good benefits.

I also witnessed two employees being arrested in the Post Office for running numbers, an illegal but popular gambling system, especially among the poor. They were excellent workers, but their lives were ruined. The difference in the lotteries and casinos of today and the gambling methods of the past is the money the government receives, not the morality of gambling.

The numbers racket seeped its way into many black and other poor communities as an undercover and tax-free means for both the gambler and the racketeer to make money. The racketeer would randomly select a set of three or four digits for the bettor to match. The bettor could place as little as a dime or up to as much as he wanted, to bet the digits he selected would match a pre-selected published number. The operation was similar to the stock market index or racetrack handle. If he won, he could make up to 600 to 1. If he lost, the racketeer would keep a portion of the money, and pay the "bookie," or collector of the numbers and money from the bettor, a small portion of the proceeds.

The communities prospered somewhat because the money remained with us. The numbers also provided a good communication system for us. It helped us to be in touch with one another, as not many could afford a telephone.

Slot machines and the lottery, however, caused a severe loss of revenue remaining in the poor community. This prevented many blacks from going into business or buying a home because the banks would not give them loans.

My father-in-law showed me a paper bag full of money that he and a numbers kingpin would take to the police station once a week and pay them to ignore the illegal activities of the numbers runners.

One of my uncles, a tall, well-built, no-nonsense hustler, ran numbers in his East Baltimore neighborhood and at Bethlehem Steel where he worked. I don't know how he managed it, but he rarely made good on his customers when they hit. He must have used his good looks to charm women out of their winnings, and his burly frame to swindle men out of theirs.

I played the numbers for about a month one year, and knew better than to trust my uncle with a penny of my money. So, Louise's Uncle Hack, who had been working at Bethlehem Steel for more than twenty years, would stop by my house and collect my bet. He collected for many people in Turners Station, including my mother. The only day I hit, along with my mother, was the day he got caught on his job at the Point for writing numbers there, and was fired. He remained heartbroken for the rest of his life, and six years later, died of lung cancer at age fifty-six. I didn't even get paid and have not played a number since.

After working at the Post Office for about a month, about twenty of us were talking while we filed mail. Although we were all sitting no more than three feet apart, and everyone was talking, the supervisor singled me out and demanded that I stop. Looking around, I inadvertently mentioned that everyone was talking and working at the same time. Then a coworker said something and I responded.

"I told you to stop talking!" the supervisor yelled.

Before I knew it and without thinking, I said, "If you would do some work yourself, you wouldn't just see me talking."

The very next day, another supervisor approached me. "I'm just the man to fire you," he snapped, without reason.

I thought to myself, I've got a wife and two kids and am buying a home. I can't afford to lose my job yet.

Several months later, a different supervisor quietly approached me. "I see you work well, and I know the other supervisor doesn't like you, but I have a special job for you, if you like."

The responsibilities included changing the time on twelve machines every half hour, and then retrieving the air mail and special delivery for a specific type of stamping, reflecting month, day, and time. I welcomed the job and never spoke with another supervisor on that floor for more than a year.

By then, I was confident that my job was secure. That was until one day, I left an air mail letter in a case, and because it was so small, I couldn't see it right away. It was a complete oversight. The same supervisor, who had hollered at me months earlier, now walked past me and called me "dumb" for having overlooked the letter. Since he was no longer my supervisor, I caught up to him and said in my own way, "Let's go outside so I can send you to your next life."

I knew fighting on the premises meant immediate discharge, but I was mad enough to take my chances. He wasn't, though, and never bothered me again.

This particular supervisor had fired more blacks than all the other supervisors combined. His all-black crew would secretly complain about his demeaning behavior, to no avail. Publicly, though, they would always be seen laughing and joking with him, although it was obvious he was not fond of them.

After a couple of years, the administration encouraged the supervisor to retire. The same black employees who had complained about him got together and bought him the biggest television available at the time. Most of them had also served in WWII, but had not had the Tuskegee experience. They could serve in supporting roles in all-black units during the war without becoming officers. The Tuskegee Airmen had a greater sense of pride and strength. I had become too busy to even discuss my own wartime experience. I had, however, learned the mentality and behavior of those I considered "Uncle Toms."

I became fast friends with a coworker and fellow Tuskegee Airman named Harry White. He was a very calm person, not easily ruffled. Sometimes he treated a couple of us to a club and dinner. After six months, he told me he couldn't work in a place like the Post Office anymore, and joined the Baltimore City Police Force. Because I had a young family, I couldn't afford to leave and take a pay cut. When I saw him again a few weeks later, he had married and was still looking very cool, calm, and collected.

FAMILY DYNAMICS

After several years as a sub, I finally became a permanent employee. My position at the Post Office had become more secure, but my family life was slowly malfunctioning, especially with so many family members meddling.

Louise's mother and my parents had not stopped trying to control us. When she got pregnant for the third time, I met with everyone and made the announcement.

"I'm taking off for thirty days," I said. "This baby is mine. I will raise this one. Don't bother me and don't visit unless I tell you. I'm going to feed and take care of it." I made sure both families knew I was going to run my own home.

Louise and I decided that if we had a girl, we would name her Velda. When our daughter was born, I raced to the hospital, only to hear Mrs. Tyler declare that she wanted another name for the baby. I held my ground and said we would name the baby as planned. Louise timidly sided with her mother and as a result of the confusion, confined herself to her bed with crying fits for more than a month.

When Linda and Janet were born, Louise would recuperate at her mother's each time for close to two months, as was required by old folks in those days. But this time, I stayed home for the next month and kept my family with me. I hand-washed the baby's cloth diapers and hung them up myself. I started cooking, although I'd never cooked a meal in my life.

Thirty minutes before the baby was hungry, I would prepare the bottle. When she started fidgeting with her fingers, I'd dry her real fast and give her the bottle. When she was finished, I'd burp her and dry her again. In the middle of the night, I would set a warm bottle by the bed about a half hour before she even whimpered. When she made the least sound, I'd pick her up, dry her, and give her that bottle. I'd burp and dry her again, and she'd go right back to sleep. She rarely cried for anything.

Five months into her little life, we still could not agree on a name. So, we called her, "Baby." Linda, by now quite bubbly and fun-loving, was in first grade. Janet, however, was still home and apparently affected by the adversity.

One day, Louise left Janet and Baby home while she went across the street to the store. Janet picked up a hairbrush, reached as far as she could through the rails of the crib and gave Baby a whipping. When Louise returned, Baby was screaming at the top of her lungs. Bristle marks covered her face and arms. That's when Janet received the biggest whipping of her little life, and Louise felt bad enough to buy her a couple of doughnuts. She got Baby settled, and propped Janet in front of the window so she could watch out for Linda coming home from school, hoping to distract her while she ran back to the store and bought those doughnuts. But that was not to be. As soon as she left, Janet picked the brush up again and woke Baby up with another face lashing. Louise could hear her from around the corner. She ran into the house, dropped the box of doughnuts, and spanked Janet again. With the two children still screaming, Louise picked Baby up and set the box of doughnuts on Janet's lap, allowing her to eat as many as she wanted. Janet never touched Baby again.

Louise and I tried hard to name Baby as soon as possible so that the tension would ease in the home and our lives. It took a couple of years, but we finally named her Sheila Debra Louise Holmes.

AROUND 1925

MOTHER, LILLIE HOLMES, 21 YEARS OLD
FATHER, JOSEPH HOLMES, ABOUT 35 YEARS OLD
BROTHER, LLOYD, 2 YEARS OLD

1952
GRAND UNCLE MOSES SANDERS AND SISTER,
GRANDMOTHER ROSA EVA JOYNER

ALLEGEDLY, THEIR PARENTS WERE WHITE AND INDIAN

1952
COMRADES – FUNDRAISER TO PROVIDE ASSISTANCE
TO THOSE IN NEED

LEFT TO RIGHT: SAMUEL (SJ) JOHNSON, TILESTON VENABLE, ELLWOOD MACKLIN, ST. CLAIR RANDOLPH, JOHN SPEED. HOWARD FLOURNOY, QUINCY MICKEY, WILLIAM ADAMS, MILTON HOLMES, WILLIAM NEAL, JACKSON, ROY WAGSTAFF, HARRY ANDERSON, CHARLES VENABLE, EDDIE JOE HOLLOWAY, BENJAMIN JONES

Turner Station Club Aids Fire Victims

The Comrades Social and Athletic Club of Turner Station through John Speed Jr., treasurer, here presents a check for $180 to Mr. and Mrs. Samuel Major whose home was destroyed by fire a few weeks ago. Other club members looking on are left to right, Benjamin Jones, vice-president; Milton Holmes, business manager; Tileston Veneble, president; and Eddie Holloway, chaplain.

NATIONAL ALLIANCE OF POSTAL EMPLOYEES (NAPE) MEMBERS AT A MARCH ON WASHINGTON

CHRISTMAS 1964
BASKETS FOR THE NEEDY
LOADING OVER 100 BASKETS OF FOOD THAT WERE ASSEMBLED
IN THE BASEMENT OF MY HOME
LEFT TO RIGHT: DAUGHTERS SHEILA, 10, AND MICHELE, 7, JACE WOODS, MILTON HOLMES, NAPE CHAIRPERSON PUBLIC RELATIONS, JOHN WHITE, NAPE PRESIDENT, JOHN GRAY, MOSES CANADA, LEVY DOZIER, WILLIAM GOODWIN, ARTHUR CARTER NAPE PUBLIC RELATIONS COMMITTEE MEMBERS

FIRST STAFF TARGET CITY YOUTH PROGRAM (TCYP)DANNY GANT, TEAM LEADER, FRANK TILLMAN-INSTRUCTOR, FRANK PULLEN-COUNSELOR,ROY MOODY-TEAM LEADER, FRANK BOONE-COUNSELOR, JERRY SAMUELS-TEAM LEADER, SITTING-MILTON HOLMES-DIRECTOR, ANGUA MARTIN-SECRETARY

1969
GRADUATION CEREMONY AT DUNBAR HIGH SCHOOL, BALTIMORE, MD
(MY ALMA MATER)
DRESSED IN DASHIKIS TO SYMBOLIZE THE CIVIL RIGHTS MOVEMENT
AND THE LIFE OF DR. MARTIN LUTHER KING JR.

1983

RECEIVING A PLAQUE FROM
THE DIRECTOR OF HISPANIC AFFAIRS

STAFF, FOUR OF WHOM ARE HISPANIC,
ARE PRESENT AT THE PRESENTATION

WEDDING ESCORT, HOWARD ALLMOND, JACKIE'S UNCLE, PASSED AWAY TWO MONTHS AFTER OUR WEDDING

1984
OUR FAMILY WEDDING PICTURE (REDUCED)

TOP: RONALD (SON-IN-LAW) WITH GRANDSON EUVON, NEXT ROW: ERICA, NIECE; JEANNE HAWKES, COUSIN; MICHELE AND SHEILA, DAUGHTERS; SHELLY, COUSIN

SECOND ROW: JANET AND LINDA, DAUGHTERS; FLORENCE, SISTER FRONT ROW: PARTIALLY VISIBLE MARGO, DAUGHTER, MICHAEL, GRANDSON; ROLAND, SON, BRIDE AND GROOM; GAIL, SISTER

ST PETER'S CHURCH IN AMSTERDAM, HOLLAND
JACKIE AND I VISITED HOLLAND ON A TRIP SPONSORED BY
THE NEW BRUNSWICK THEOLOGICAL SEMINARY TO STUDY
AT THE UNIVERSITY OF LEIDEN. THE WORKSHOPS INCLUDED
LECTURES BY RELIGIOUS LEADERS OF DIFFERENT
FAITHS ON 'SUFFERING AND SALVATION'.

JACKIE AND I PRESENT PLAQUE TO PETER ANGELOS

ON BEHALF OF THE ROYAL EXTENDED FAMILY, A NONPROFIT CORPORATION,

FOR HIS LEADERSHIP IN 1962 TO SECURE

THE PASSAGE OF THE PUBLIC ACCOMMODATIONS BILL IN

BALTIMORE, MARYLAND.

MR. ANGELOS IS THE OWNER OF THE BALTIMORE ORIOLES BASEBALL TEAM.

1987
LOS ANGELES, CALIFORNIA

VISITING DAUGHTER, JANET AND SON-IN-LAW, EUVON JONES: CHILDREN MARGUERITE, 14 YRS. OLD, ROLAND, 10 YRS. OLD AND GRANDSON, ROBERT, 4YRS. OLD

1989

TWENTY-SEVEN YOUNG RELATIVES VISITED
OUR HOME FOR TWO WEEKS

LIL'AL-ROLAND-KEISHA-ASHLEY-MARGO-LIL SMITTY-ANGELA-JESSICA-
CHARISMA-CRISTINA-NEHEMIAH-TAMMY-JEREMY-SIMONE-DANIELE-TRAVIS-
T'HAI-ROBERT-EUVON-JOSEPH-LEE J-ALEXIE

LIL ROD-KELLY-CRISTAL-MELODY-JACQUETTA

BROTHER JOHN MUHAMMAD ATTENDED WORSHIP SERVICE AT
ALLEN CHAPEL AME CHURCH
HE AND HIS MEMBERS HELD THEIR MEETINGS IN THE CHURCH
FOR SEVERAL MONTHS WHILE
THEIR FACILITIES WERE BEING RENOVATED

DR. JOSEPHINE YOUNG-O'NEAL TEACHING CLASS:
THE STAGES AND ART OF COUNSELING

1993

EARNED DR. OF MINISTRY AT DREW UNIVERSITY
AT SIXTY-SEVEN YEARS OF AGE

1975

DAUGHTER, JANET JONES, GRADUATING WITH
A DEGREE IN ENGLISH LITERATURE, FROM
MORGAN STATE UNIVERSITY

2008

GRANDSON, EUVON JONES, GRADUATING
WITH A DEGREE IN BUSINESS ADMINISTRATION
FROM BOWIE STATE UNIVERSITY

1995

MILLION MAN MARCH IN WASHINGTON, D.C.
ORGANIZED BY THE HONORABLE LOUIS FARRAKHAN

SEPTEMBER 1970

CELEBRATING DADDY'S 80TH BIRTHDAY
LEFT TO RIGHT: MYSELF, AGE 44-UNCLE LESLIE JOYNER,
60-SISTER ROSA JANE, 34-SISTER ODESSA,40-FRED, 38
ABSENT DELMUS, 22

FIVE DAUGHTERS OF FIRST MARRIAGE
SHEILA-ANGELA-JANET-MICHELE-LINDA
LINDA, THE OLDEST, PASSED IN 2000

GRANDSON, EUVON, WITH GREAT GRANDCHILDREN

JORDAN BABBS-TYLIND JONES-RYEN BABBS

HARRY PUGH (Hicky)-MYSELF-ROOSEVELT TYLER (Zack)

OVER 60 YEARS FRIENDSHIP-2011

GRANDCHILDREN
BACK ROW: RONALD SMITH JR. - EUVON JONES - ROBERT MOORE JR - FRONT ROW: T'HAI JONES - CRISTINA JONES - ALEXIE SMITH

DAUGHTER, MICHELE, GRADUATING
WITH A DEGREE IN NURSING, WITH SON, RAPHAEL

DAUGHTER, SHEILA SMITH, GRADUATING WITH A DEGREE IN NURSING
FROM COPPIN STATE UNIVERSITY IN BALTIMORE, MARYLAND -
SHE IS ESCORTED BY HUSBAND RONALD AND SON RONALD JR

SON, ROLAND BROOKS-ATTORNEY, BALTIMORE, MD.

JACKIE AND I CONGRATULATE DAUGHTER MARGUERITE

AS SHE RECEIVES HER PHD IN NURSING AT THE UNIVERSITY OF PENNSYLVANIA. GRANDSON NOAH PROUDLY OBSERVED THE CEREMONY

RECOGNITION OF TINTON FALLS MEMBER DAVID LEGG FOR HIS VISITS TO SOUTH AMERICA TO ASSIST IN DEVELOPING PROJECTS FOR CLEAN WATER

GRANDSON, EUVON, AND I AT THE

2009 INAUGURATION, PRESIDENT BARACK OBAMA

RUSSELL ANDERSON AND I DISCUSS THE CONSTRUCTION OF THE GAZEBO DONATED BY THE TINTON ROTARY CLUB TO THE WEST PARK AVENUE PARK IN TINTON FALLS

DELIVERING A SPEECH FOR BLACK HISTORY MONTH
TURNERS STATION, MARYLAND -2009

DAUGHTER, MICHELE, SON-IN-LAW
EUVON JONES, AND I AT THE DEDICATION
OF COMMUNITY ACTIVIST, ELSIE WINSTON

ROTARY CLUB FIVE GROUP STUDY EXCHANGE (GSE)

GUESTS FROM ARGENTINA VISIT THE TINTON FALLS, NEW JERSEY'S ROTARY CLUB CHAPTER OF DISTRICT 7500 TO OBSERVE OCCUPATIONS SIMILAR TO THEIR AREAS OF INTEREST IN ARGENTINA, SOUTH AMERICA

BACK ROW: LEFT TO RIGHT- VISITOR-DAVID LEGG, MEMBER TINTON FALLS CHAPTER, (TFC) –VISITOR

MIDDLE ROW: RUSSELL ANDERSON, (TFC)-VISITOR-GSE TEAM MEMBER-CAROL LEGG, (TFC)-VISITOR-JUDGE TONY BRUNO, (TFC)

FRONT ROW: FOUR VISITORS-TONY MALONE, (TFC)-MILTON HOLMES

2013

MY DAUGHTERS, SHEILA SMITH AND JANET JONES, DR. CHARLES MCGEE, AND I AT THE AMERICAN GLORY RECEPTION SALUTING THE TUSKEGEE AIRMEN AND CELEBRATING INAUGURATION OF PRESIDENT BARACK OBAMA

RELOCATION

A short time after successfully naming Sheila and returning to some sense of normalcy, my car fell apart. So, in December 1956, I bought a new 1957 Plymouth. Our tight two-bedroom home had also become too small for our growing family, and I decided to move out of Turners. Several other members of my club, The Comrades, had moved away as well, and I knew I would always have ties to the community because our families and close friends lived there. I just couldn't see myself remaining in that box for the rest of my life.

We accepted a down payment on our home from an older, rotund, yet jovial man named Mr. Byrd. He was so excited about buying his first house that he would periodically stop by with his enormous smile and peppy conversation to check on our moving progress. Louise, however, was anxious to remain there because she didn't want to leave her mother. But I persisted, believing we would have a better chance if we were farther away.

Finally, the day arrived for settlement. Louise and I picked up Mr. and Mrs. Byrd and drove to the Federal Housing Authority in Baltimore City to complete the transaction. They were cheerful after the sale, and Mrs. Byrd wanted to go to a furniture store. Mr. Byrd and I sat in the car and had a good conversation while our wives shopped. Afterwards, I dropped them back at their apartment to wait until we moved about two days later.

Around eleven o'clock that night, Mrs. Byrd called in tears to say that Mr. Byrd had died suddenly of a heart attack. I was shocked and saddened because I knew how much moving into our home meant to him. I dropped everything and went to visit her, asking if she wanted to void the sale. She refused, believing that he would have wanted her to enjoy the home.

I relocated my family to Northwest Baltimore and settled in the 200 block of Denison Street in a community called Edmondson Village. We were the third black family on that block of close to twenty-six families. At night and through the thin walls, we could hear our white neighbors calling us all kinds of names.

Three months later, two feet of snow fell, and the entire city was paralyzed for a week. Because we lived on a block that had a slight decline, no one could drive until the first car at the bottom of the hill was cleared enough to move. From that first house on, which was owned by another black family, we had to work together to move our cars. Soon after that, the whites began moving out in a hurry, with most gone within a year.

In the meantime, Louise almost had a nervous breakdown because she could hardly bear to be away from her mother. We were then about twenty miles away; yet, we visited them at least twice a week when we attended Wednesday night choir rehearsal at our church, and Sunday morning worship service. It was still not enough. She was so strongly controlled by Mrs. Tyler that she couldn't function properly without her. In consideration of the children, I decided to be more patient and work with her, but by then, we had another girl and had a much easier time naming her Michele.

With Louise preoccupied with Sheila and Michele, I took a more active role in Linda and Janet's education. I joined the Parent Teacher Association and soon became president. At the first meeting, there was more than $3,100 in the treasury that the white families had accumulated through fund raising. Within two years, the treasury had dwindled to $300. Blacks just didn't have the funds or programs to augment the treasury. We even held committee meetings in family homes, but funds were never available. With our limited ability to service our children's education, these meetings became a charade, masking a deeper need to continue the quality of education that was consistent with surrounding white communities.

I eventually had to relinquish much of my formal involvement with the PTA because with a new car, new house, and new daughter, I needed a second job.

TAXI DRIVER

As a taxi driver, the rule was that I would have to drive at least twenty hours each week in order to keep my job. That was all right with me, though, because not only did I need the money, but taxi driving became a real education. I made it a point to challenge myself to see how quickly and how much I could engage each passenger to talk about him or herself. Usually, because I genuinely like people, I was successful.

It was interesting to observe the patterns and attitudes of some of the passengers I met. Since I was working the afternoon shift at the Post Office, I drove some weekday mornings and at various times on the weekends. During the week, people were rushing to get to work and were usually a bit tense. Saturday mornings and early afternoons were major shopping times, and people tended to be grateful, particularly when I helped with their packages and groceries. Friday and Saturday nights were exciting and predictable. From early evening until close to midnight, the passengers would be heading to a party or a dance, happy as larks. Between midnight and two-thirty, there was much alcohol-induced chatter and exhilaration. Then, a couple hours later, before sunrise, guys would be ushering their female friends into the taxi to be driven home.

Believe it or not, Sunday mornings and early afternoons were the most depressing. First, passengers were seemingly more tense and argumentative on their way to church than those on their way to work during the week. Second, those who rode in the taxi seemed even more disturbed or angry after they left church than those who had taken a taxi to get to church. Third, police assistance was always available to direct traffic for the white churches, but never for the black ones.

Whenever I worked on Sundays, some of us drivers would discuss those issues, and I tried to avoid working then. There were times, though, I had no choice because I had to earn my twenty hours. I resigned after five years because I had become very active in the labor union and the Civil Rights movement.

THE URGE TO REBEL

The black postal workers tried to adjust to discrimination with a positive attitude, and we tried to have fun. Three of us close friends approached the superintendent of the afternoon shift one day and requested that we be permitted to work thirteen days straight, if we could have every other Sunday off. He agreed to our proposal, and we worked that schedule for two and a half years, except during the Christmas season, when the requirement was seven days a week. Once I became a regular employee, my days of overtime were over, except for the three to four weeks during Christmas.

Some of us played pinochle every lunch hour. We played hard and fast to see if we could complete three games in one half hour. I also had a little fun organizing a bowling league. There were only two bowling alleys with duck pins, but we had just as much fun. I also organized a softball team to play several other industries that had also established softball teams.

I came to a point in my professional life where I wondered where my future was headed. I also wondered where my people were going? It was obvious that discrimination was as rampant in the Post Office as in the community around us. Out of almost 300 supervisors and upper management employees, only three were black, and two of them were in the parcel post station.

To file the mail that was to be sent on the right trains to the right cities required so much study and scheme recollection that you had to be tested annually. Passing the scheme annually was easier if you had the opportunity to work during the year in the area where that knowledge was necessary. Most blacks, however, were not permitted to work there. That meant that you had to study harder each year to pass the test, even if you didn't get a chance to practice your skill during the year.

I stopped playing pinochle and began reading everything I could about the Civil War. I wanted to know how a minority, as was the Confederacy, could fight so long against the overwhelming North and its vast resources. After reading volumes about the Confederacy and Robert E. Lee, I read a lot about the Union. I concluded that the South was more dedicated to its cause, better organized, and guided by more efficient leadership on the battlefield.

With the limited time I had, I began taking some self-improvement courses, one at a time. Simultaneously, discrimination became more disturbing to me.

In the Post Office, white employees belonged to a separate union for each craft and had members in all of them, including the supervisors, clerks, carriers, mail handlers, motor vehicle service workers, and special delivery messengers.

Blacks were excluded from participating in any one of those unions. So, they formed their own organization called The National Alliance of Postal Employees. Eventually, membership was expanded to include all crafts.

The National Alliance of Postal Employees was the first industrial union in the country of which I became an active member.

THE REBELLION BEGINS

I engaged in my first fight in 1960 when the president of the National Alliance, John White, requested that I attend one of its meetings. People were needed to support the NAACP. College students were picketing, and sit-ins had erupted in North Carolina, gradually spreading to other states, particularly Maryland. These young people were being arrested on a daily basis. The NAACP had to use a couple of its lawyers to help bail them out and pay some of their legal fees. For this purpose, the NAACP solicited funds from churches and other citizens groups around Baltimore City. Since the church parishioners were donating a lot of the money, the ministers were dogged in their attempt to take control of it away from the NAACP.

A huge meeting involving community leaders, the NAACP, and ministers was called. John White, five other Alliance members, and I attended the meeting. An argument arose about who was going to handle the money. With little else being accomplished, the attendees decided to have another meeting. During the second meeting, there was still a barrage of excessive verbal hostility and unresolved issues regarding financial control of monies collected to help the students.

After some maneuvering and strategizing, John White became president of the NAACP Student Non-Violent Coordinating Committee. He suggested that the wisest thing to do would be to form a committee to conduct a study and bring a recommendation back to the body. I was appointed to the committee of five to present a recommendation at the next meeting.

We met at a Bishop's office. One of the ministers who showed up was not a committee member. He took over the meeting and, while the rest of the group was trying to make a decision about the distribution of money, he ranted about allegations he had heard about the NAACP, and about the rumor that the president's son was an alcoholic. It seemed to me nothing more than a power struggle and a personal vendetta to divert the committee's attention.

Finally, based on his accusations, a recommendation was made that the money would go to the ministers. I voted against that proposal and informed John White that I didn't know what to do. He said they probably used the *Robert's Rules of Order* to control the vote. I had never heard of that book before.

I checked it out of the library and read it all night long. Finally, I read something about a minority report, in which one or more members can put in writing a separate report as a substitute motion for the report by the majority on the committee.

When we met again, the committee chairman gave his report that the committee recommended the funds be turned over to the ministers, and he made a motion to that effect. The presiding officer stated the motion and asked, "Are you ready for the question?"

I immediately responded that I was not ready and presented in writing my substitute motion that the funds raised for the NAACP Student Non-Violent Coordinating Committee be received and dispersed by the NAACP Baltimore Branch. The motion passed because we had packed the meeting with National Alliance members.

When the meeting adjourned, the leader of the ministers said gruffly, "You can kiss my ass," and walked out.

My experiences convinced me that many ministers had ulterior motives and their own agendas, particularly where money was concerned.

I was now formally involved in the Civil Rights Movement.

MY COMMITMENT TO CIVIL RIGHTS

After that success, John White invited me to a National Alliance of Postal Employees branch meeting and named me Public Relations Chairman, which meant that I was on the board. I asked the older guys what the duties were. They responded that all we had to do was meet three times a year. I went to the library and borrowed some books on public relations, and John took a similar course at Johns Hopkins University. I learned then how important public relations are to an organization.

When I attended my first Alliance board meeting, I had nothing to contribute. So I listened in to learn. At the second meeting, when they discussed an issue, every time I opened my mouth to comment, they called me "out of order." Nobody advised me how to make a motion. I didn't know what to say or when to say it. I was out of order all night. I had comments and opinions, but couldn't express them. When the meeting adjourned and we got ready to eat, I cussed them all out.

"I'll get y'all one of these days. Y'all don't have any sense anyway, and you don't know how to treat someone who's new."

A few days later, during a postal training session at work, I told a friend, Lou Clemens, about the meeting. He advised that I needed to know more about Parliamentary Procedure. I needed to apply more of what I had gleaned from reading *Robert's Rules of Order*.

"Can you help me out?" I asked.

"Sure," he said. "There's a lawyer here by the name of Joe Zeller. He teaches it. I'll tell you what. We have to have at least ten in the class. I'll organize some guys, you get one or two, and we'll take the class. It takes about ten sessions, and he'll be glad to teach it."

I invited a letter carrier, Leon Proctor, to take the class with me. We attended those sessions of Parliamentary Procedure taught by this attorney, and by the time summer was over, we were back at the board meeting. They couldn't tell me anything about the subject after that. If anyone intimated that I was out of order, I would refer to the page, paragraph, and the line to prove otherwise. I began taking over. Subsequently, people got jealous, accusing me of being a firebrand, but I didn't care. I ran for second vice president and won.

I was also named to a by-law committee. In that position, I realized we needed to raise dues to be more effective. We did so three times in five years. Each time the by-laws were amended, it included a raise in dues. I would attend each meeting of the committees to explain my objective and seek support. Each proposed change was accepted without much conflict.

In 1960, we raised dues to encourage more members and their families to attend our annual national convention.

The second raise in dues was to allow the president to be paid when off the clock to handle a complaint or grievance case. It was also critical for us to buy a building. As the Alliance grew, I knew we would need more office space, meeting rooms, and a kitchen.

When I attended my first Branch meeting, they were being held in the YMCA. The environment was subdued, with only about fifteen members attending, and we were paying $20 per meeting.

So I got permission to look for another place and soon found one in the Mondawmin Shopping Center, right in the center of Baltimore City. There was enough space for more than 150 people. Food and drinks were allowed, all at no cost. The facility was available for our Branch meetings once a month, but not for committee meetings.

It was agreed again that I could look for a building to procure so we could have more control over our environment and meeting times. I found one, and although there were eighteen members on the board, John White and I were the only ones who volunteered to put our homes up as collateral for the loan we would need to secure the building. We successfully bought the facility and paid the loan off in ten years, as agreed.

The third raise in 1964 was to pay the president to be available on a full-time basis. The larger the Alliance grew, so did John's commitment.

I became very close to the Alliance and would handle many cases regarding employees who had been unfairly disciplined in some way. I was also a principal writer of the Alliance newsletter, which was published and distributed monthly. I was truly dedicated to the work.

PUBLIC RELATIONS

After being designated chairperson of the Public Relations Committee, I soon learned that I had to actually form the committee myself. I took my time and formed a committee of seven dedicated colleagues, including myself, who represented other crafts besides clerks. The main Post Office, where I worked, operated twenty-four hours a day and encompassed three shifts.

I encouraged John Gray to be the representative on the first shift in the main Post Office, Moses Canada on the second shift, and Arthur Carter on the third. Levy Dozier was selected to represent the mail handlers. Leon Proctor was the advocate for the letter handlers, and Sam Goodwin spoke for the motor vehicle service.

I immediately took a short course in leadership, which emphasized that the chief functions of a leader are to plan, organize, direct, and control.

Having organized the committee, we held our first meeting in October 1960. We agreed on three projects for the following year to make the Alliance more visible in the community, and to provide a community service, particularly for the poor. We in the Post Office were securely employed with middle class incomes.

First, we would request that the Alliance give the president a testimonial dinner because under his leadership, the number of members had increased from about 300 to almost 1,000 within a seven-year period. Surely that should not be a problem.

Next, we would sponsor a raffle to raise funds to increase what was already in the treasury. Then we proposed another modest raise in the dues.

Finally, during the Christmas holidays, we would sponsor a Basket for the Needy Program for the disadvantaged in the community.

The proposals were submitted at the Board's next meeting.

I was informed that I had to get permission from Ed Fisher, the director of Welfare, and purportedly John White's right hand man, to proceed with the testimonial. I was also informed that a raffle was illegal. The third problem was there weren't any funds for making baskets for the needy.

A few days later, after I had cooled down from a fit of anger, I approached Mr. Fisher, who finally agreed it was all right because he didn't have the time (even though he was asked to have the testimonial two years prior). I went to the permit section of the police station and secured a permit for the raffle.

The following Board meeting was rather short in comparison to the previous one. The proposals now had to be approved at a regular meeting of the Branch. Three of the proposals; the increase in dues, the permit for a raffle, and the Basket for the Needy Program were easily approved. However, when the item for a testimonial dinner for the president was opened for discussion, the president had to vacate the presiding chair and leave the room. Mr. Fisher organized and led the opposition to the affair. My committee was determined that we would fight all night long if necessary. The issue was discussed for almost two hours. After everyone, except my committee, had become weary, the testimonial was approved.

The members then voted to buy the president a modern record player for $225.

As a concession, we agreed that Mr. Fisher would be given the funds to purchase the gift and present it at the affair, which was held on a Sunday at a motel in East Baltimore, about six blocks from Mr. Fisher's home. My home was about four miles from the motel. Early in the morning, on the day of the affair, he called to inform me that if I wanted the gift to be taken to the affair and presented, I would have to come to his house and take the gift myself. I was livid, but I did it. In spite of all the obstacles, the testimonial turned out to be tremendous. More than 200 people attended, including postal officials and politicians. It improved our image and brought financial success. Mr. Fisher was quite pleasant at the beginning of the evening, but later became reserved and icy.

The following year, when the Alliance held our annual dance at the Baltimore Coliseum, Ed Fisher exploded in a fit of anger and was boisterous in his criticism of John White's wife, Betty, and her family. Betty's grandfather was a former slave who had two of his fingers severed after he was discovered reading. Her father was a railroad postal clerk who, with his wife, had six children. Betty and her two sisters earned master's degrees and were public school teachers. Her three brothers were doctors, one of whom was Percy Julian, an internationally recognized scientist known for synthesizing cortisone, testosterone, and progesterone, as well as formulating a drug to treat glaucoma. Another brother, Emerson, practiced medical care in one of the poorest sections of Baltimore City that housed a high percentage of welfare recipients. He even moved his family into the area and maintained his office in the basement of his home, which allowed him to see a high volume of patients who could easily walk into his office. He was also our family physician for many years. The third brother, James Julian, had his practice in an area consisting predominately of middle class home owners.

For about twenty minutes, Fisher ranted and criticized Mrs. White and her brothers. John never said a word, which I couldn't understand. He later explained that he did not want an altercation, which would jeopardize the reputation of the Alliance.

I had been taught in some of our workshops that every leader needs a hatchet man to protect him, and to maintain the positive image of the organization. I took that position upon myself, forcing Mr. Fisher to resign from his position in the Alliance.

Some months later, Fisher had nerve enough to seek John's support in acquiring some official position. John agreed – something else I couldn't understand – and Fisher was appointed.

Ed Fisher was a heavy smoker. About ten months later, he was diagnosed with lung cancer and soon died. He had become rather popular while in his position in the Alliance. Some of my coworkers asked me if I was going to his funeral. I gave my best polite negative response.

Meanwhile, I persuaded a friend of mine to accept the position of welfare director. As fanatics of the Baltimore Colts football team, we had become friends. That was when Johnny Unitas, Lenny Moore, Jim Parker, and Raymond Berry were on the team. When they won the Super Bowl in 1958, which revolutionized the game, we became hooked like addicts. We had an agreement with management that whenever we were scheduled to work on a Sunday, and the Baltimore Colts had a home game, we could take two hours annual leave and skip out early.

Stadium parking was always a problem on 33rd Street. We paid a coworker to sacrifice his lunch hour and take us to the game, and then return to work. We were so caught up that we would travel forty miles during the week when we had a day off to see them practice at Westminster College. Three of my neighbors and I bought season tickets to sit in the upper deck, which was the best we could do. We didn't care if we scorched in the heat of summer or froze in winter. We rotated hosting football parties and Super Bowl celebrations at our homes. I was so addicted to the sport that I only missed two home games in nineteen years.

FOOD FOR THE NEEDY

The following year, approximately 500 members and guests attended the Alliance annual dinner-dance. The great Lionel Hampton and his band were the musicians for this particular evening. Our committee decided it would be a good idea to have the baskets of food at the dance as an awareness and publicity gesture. We had requested that each attendee bring at least one can of food for the baskets. The members and guests cooperated without question.

Each year after that, all we had to do was send a note to each location requesting donations for the baskets. We always had enough funds for 100 baskets of food. Area bakeries would donate at least 300 loaves of bread.

Poor blacks, as well as whites, looked the same to us. We delivered food to families of both races. I would sometimes take my two oldest daughters, Linda and Janet, with me as I delivered the baskets. Those were the days when few people had telephones at home, which made it difficult to give notice that I would be stopping by. Yet, many times, someone would be at his or her door waiting for the gift. Usually, the baskets contained food for a Christmas Day feast, including a twelve- to twenty-five-pound turkey, a ham, yams, white potatoes, three loaves of bread, ingredients for dressing, cabbage, canned goods, and more. Most of the time, we gathered and sorted all the food in the basement of either a committee member's home, or my own. There would be about five to eight of us packing those baskets in our cars and delivering them to the families. This meant that each of us had to make multiple trips before the meats thawed.

In those moments, we thanked God for those who had donated food and funds, and the fact that we were fortunate to be able to give rather than receive. When I get the opportunity to look closely at another person's worn-out sheets, I am reminded how grateful I am for what God has provided for me and my family.

There is a saying, "But for the grace of God, there go I."

A CHANGE IN EMOTION

One of the turning points that pushed me forward in advancing civil rights at the Post Office was a confrontation with a white supervisor who was transferred to our predominately black floor. The rumor mill had circulated that he was threatening to break up the Alliance and discipline most of us. So when this tall, white-haired, well-built man appeared in our section, I wanted to get a feel for his attitude. I made it a point to go to the Post Office early because the rule was that one could walk on the floor provided one had not yet punched the clock. Once you hit the clock, it was time to work. I walked around with a bun in my hand where other people were working. As I stood in the corner, he approached me.

"Stop eating that bun." He demanded, hostilely.

I looked at him dead in the eye, "Man, I'm not on the *god-durn* clock. Leave me alone."

He moved on but kept his eye on me the rest of the day. I then wrote a nice article about him in the Alliance newsletter a couple of days later.

I wrote: "Friday the 13th was a red letter day in the mailing division of the Baltimore Post Office. On that day, the person we have come to know as 'Co-cheese' stepped on that floor with rancor in his mouth and disdain in his eyes."

Without mentioning his name, I went on to list a number of things he had done. I had 1,000 copies printed. The next day, I arrived at work at six o'clock in the morning, even though I wasn't due to report until an hour later, and put a copy in front of everyone and on every desk around. Everyone stopped working to read that article.

After that, I made it a point when I got to work to walk up to him, look him dead in the eye, and greet him.

"Good morning to you," I'd say.

Before he could answer, I'd keep right on moving. Not long after that, he was transferred to the windowless basement. There were guys down there, black and white, who did not belong to any union, who had to file large envelopes called flat mail.

One day, an angry, nervous black employee came rushing up from the basement. He said the supervisor, whom I nicknamed 'Co-cheese,' had written him up, proposing that he be terminated. This meant that if an employee were to be fired from a government job, it would be difficult, if not impossible, to be employed by the federal government again. I marched downstairs, all hyped up. I fussed hard for a while until he said he would rethink his position. The employee was not a member of the Alliance or any union, but at first I didn't care. When I saw him later, he agreed to become a member. He was not fired but, instead, suspended for three days.

About two days later, another employee came from the same area complaining that the supervisor was proposing to discipline him as well. Once again, I hurried downstairs, all excited. 'Co-cheese' pointed his finger at me. He challenged me to step outside the door. So I did, ready for a fight. But he had a strategy. He informed me that none of the employees under his supervision, black nor white, belonged to either union. He proposed that each time he threatened to discipline an employee I was to come down and sign the guy in my union as a member, fuss a bit, and he would reduce the penalty. I said to myself. "The white man is smart." I signed all the blacks in the basement.

From that point on, I made an effort to be more pragmatic than emotional. I knew I had a lot to learn about control under pressure. I realized that some white men knew more about negotiation and finesse than I.

After 'Co-cheese' retired about five years later, and I had left the Post Office, we happened to meet in downtown Baltimore. We shook hands. He smiled and said, "We sure had some fun, didn't we?"

We laughed and, after a few more pleasantries, separated. I realized that age and experience had improved our tolerance level.

EQUAL REPRESENTATION

The National Alliance held its own annual convention. I introduced a resolution to our branch, requiring that we select delegates to the national conventions by crafts in order for other positions to be represented besides clerks. It passed. Then, we delegates from Baltimore introduced the idea to the National Convention, and it passed as a policy for all branches in the country. We also launched a campaign inside the Post Office to employ more blacks. Subsequently, we frequently fought for equal recognition among the unions.

When John F. Kennedy became president, he issued Executive Order 10988, which gave us recognition among labor unions in the federal government. As a result, we had to have an election, since we needed exclusive recognition in at least one craft to be at the bargaining table. If not, we knew management and the white unions would collude together. Because of the election, the only way we could get exclusive recognition was through the mail handlers because they were predominantly black. We couldn't get recognition in any other job category.

In the process of the long election, we didn't win over the clerks, although the majority of our members were clerks, and the others were carriers. The smallest group was mail handlers, predominately black, and they joined us. We now had exclusive recognition, along with six other unions, which allowed us to approach the bargaining table with management and the other unions.

We were there to negotiate the first contract because we represented the mail handlers. On the team, I was joined by John White and Joe Dixon, the director of Welfare. John and I would negotiate, and Joe would observe.

All of a sudden, several black females were crying because they had to load thirty-pound, forty-pound, and fifty-pound bags onto trucks by themselves. Their supervisors were forcing them to do hard labor. Apparently, they were told the Equal Pay Law had passed and interpreted it to mean equal work for equal pay at the insistence of the white man. One of the ladies shed tears when we went to see the postmaster to discuss the fact that these women had been working there for twenty years. Although they had gotten older, they were still required to do this type of labor. He said there was nothing he could do, that his hands were tied. The law had been passed and the unions were pressing the issue.

John White agreed to meet at my house that night. We sat down with a fifth of whiskey and tried to figure out what to do. After almost seven hours of brainstorming, I had an idea. We would write a counter-proposal stating that women should have equal access to promotion for equal pay, as well as supervisors, as they were required to do equal work. No woman had ever been promoted to a supervisory position. We had it typed up and made copies.

At our negotiating session the next morning, when we set a copy in front of everyone, you could hear a feather float. There were only three blacks in the crowded room. They looked at us; the unions objected to what we had proposed. Management said it couldn't do anything with the law that was passed. We insisted that if we have equal work for equal pay, we must have equal promotion. The whites began fighting amongst themselves.

Although the predominately black females had been working in the Post Office since WWII, not one was even considered for a higher position. After that session, the subtle harassment ceased.

About three years later, the unions and management renegotiated the contract. I was the spokesperson for the Alliance because John White was ill and could not attend. I was now the first vice president. We were involved in approximately four days of intense negotiating for eight hours each day. At the end of one day, I returned to the section where I worked to obtain some information that would assist me in the negotiations. A black temporary acting-supervisor, who had not even passed the supervisor's exam, yelled at me almost as loud as he could.

"Why don't you get to work now!"

"Why don't you shut up and leave me alone!" I hollered back at him louder than he had at me. I was drained from having to negotiate another contract with management all day long.

It was interesting to me that when we lived in the same community, I picked the acting-supervisor up every day from his house to give him a ride to work. We always had good conversation. He was faithful in his church, and was an excellent singer. I said to myself, "Power corrupts."

Regardless of race, nationality, or sex, it's easier for a person in charge to *abuse* authority, than to be knowledgeable enough to know how to *use* it to encourage a subordinate to work efficiently. Walking in the other person's shoes rewards both persons.

SUPERVISORY EXAMINATION

When I began working in the main Post Office in 1951, the work force encompassed more than 4000 employees, about thirty percent of them black. There were also close to 300 supervisors, only three of whom were black. Those three worked in a building that processed packages and boxes only. The great majority of the employees in that building were also black. It was a dusty old building next to the Pennsylvania Railroad Station.

The National Alliance complained about the lack of black supervisors, until the Post Office Department agreed to give a written exam in supervision and management to employees who wanted to achieve that kind of leadership.

The policy was initiated by President John F. Kennedy, and continued by the Lyndon B. Johnson administration.

Once the exam was scheduled, a rule was established that the first 100 candidates with the best scores would be posted on all floors and in every one of the thirty-plus buildings. It was given at a large college. Approximately 1,500 employees took the exam, which included about 500 blacks.

When the scores were posted, there I was – number twenty. I had scored close to perfect. The next black who had scored close to 100 was around number eighty. The only person who congratulated me was my friend and mentor, John White. He scored around ninety.

I came to understand that my people, whom I had represented in certain cases, and who seemed friendly toward me, now viewed me as a complete stranger, while the whites looked at me with disdain.

During the war, when those of us who had passed the screening test, the exam to become a pilot, and then transferred to Keesler Field, Mississippi, to take the four-day exam, the other soldiers were proud of us, unlike those in the Post Office.

Although I qualified and was offered a supervisory position, I declined the promotion. I did, however, organize preparatory classes to teach other Alliance members how to pass the exam. I had all kinds of refreshments for them and offered the class at no charge. Only eight showed up.

On the other hand, the white unions set up classes for their members, and charged each one $3 to participate. It was reported that their classes were standing room only.

Considering all my experiences, I concluded that the generation of the baby boomers would produce several generations of self-centered people exhibiting insecure behavior – the "Me, Myself and I" syndrome. This entitlement generation would be capable of preventing effective development of our community.

PICKETING FOR CIVIL RIGHTS

When Governor George Wallace of Alabama came to Baltimore in the early 1960's, we took serious action. Somehow, we received word that he would be staying at a hotel in the northeastern section of Baltimore County. At the time, blacks didn't live in that affluent area.

Around three-thirty in the afternoon, one of the sons of the local president of the NAACP picked me up at the Post Office where I had just finished for the day. We drove out to Towson, where the governor would be staying, and joined about fifty others in picketing in protest of his bold discriminatory stance against James Meredith, a black college student enrolling into the University of Mississippi. He was equally resistant in allowing blacks to enroll in the University of Alabama.

In less than a half hour, nearly 200 whites, the majority being young adults, along with the Ku Klux Klan, assembled at the corner across the street with baseball bats and sticks. They were screaming and calling us all the obnoxious names they could think of. At that point, since this was supposedly a nonviolent protest, we had to resolve that we were prepared for the consequences. Luckily, the police arrived after what seemed like a small lifetime, and observed without disbursing the crowd. The hecklers thankfully calmed down just enough to avoid police response.

When the car carrying Gov. Wallace arrived, I noticed him sitting in the back passenger seat nearest the curb. I walked slowly by his vehicle and got right in his face, gazing at him. He cussed, and I kept right on staring and picketing. He let me know that I wasn't the only one who could speak another language.

What was so amazing to me was that not long after that, Gov. Wallace took a position in favor of integration, just as firmly as he had done to maintain segregation. I then concluded that too many politicians vote the conscience, if any, of the vocal minority, rather than their own. I recognized then that I could never be a politician. Based on my experiences in receiving encouragement from all sides, I knew I wanted to help those who were in need, regardless of who they were.

I have often wondered what became of those boisterous protestors of 1963. Did they, too, experience a conversion, or are they the same? That incident was more than forty-five years ago. Have any of them become city, state, or federal officials, or elected to an office? Do their descendants oppose equal opportunity, or have they wished that Hurricane Katrina was as devastating to blacks as the one in the Mississippi Valley in 1926-27, which was considered the worst flood in United States history?

Because of the programs we sponsored in the National Alliance of Postal Employees, President John White, Director of Welfare Joseph Dixon, and I, the Public Relations director, became best friends.

During that time, blacks could neither eat in the restaurants in downtown Baltimore, nor stay in any of its hotels. Even though we were not permitted to eat inside the facilities, some of our coworkers would walk to the outside window and buy a sandwich to eat during their lunch breaks. Although I was disappointed, I felt maybe as veterans of WWII, they were so trained to be willing to accept segregation in a country they had risked their lives to protect, they had lost their pride.

We three decided to picket in front of the main take-out restaurants near the Post Office. Each day at lunchtime, we took two hours annual leave. After a couple of weeks, we decided that a city ordinance would have a greater influence and prove more effective than a demonstration. In order for an ordinance to pass, it required a majority vote. The City Council consisted of twenty-one members, who were elected by the voters in their particular district. Therefore, eleven votes were required to pass an ordinance.

There was one black on the City Council at the time who was the director of Cortez Peters Business School, which offered classes to improve the communication skills of its students. The director, Councilman Dixon, and the school were well respected in the black community for the quality of its curriculum and staff. When we met with him, he advised us that he had already submitted a bill for consideration, but that he would try to amend the current law to include public accommodations.

Baltimore City had passed legislation establishing the Equal Employment Opportunity Commission; however, an amendment was necessary to delete the word "Employment," and change the title to Baltimore Equal Opportunity Commission. This change would automatically include public accommodations. When we met with one of the leaders of the City Council, who was from a district that we considered predominately Jewish, we expected his support because he frequently reminded us of his commitment to support civil rights. He also emphasized that there were four city councilmen from his district who would naturally support the change. The Jews I had interacted with had always been supportive of my efforts for inclusion. Blacks were primarily concentrated in several inner city districts. We needed seven more votes from those districts to pass legislation that would not only prohibit discrimination in employment, but also public accommodations. We recognized that it could be political suicide for a white politician from a predominately white district to vote for a public accommodations bill.

We requested that he recommend someone who may be willing to take a risk. He said there was a young, brash new person who may be helpful. His name was Peter Angelos, the current owner of the Baltimore Orioles baseball team. However, he was from a predominately white and Italian district. We made an impromptu visit with him. He seemed relaxed and said he would see what he could do. Councilman Dixon, author of the bill, made the motion for the bill to have its third and final reading before being voted on. We were appreciative for the unexpected support.

I had been meeting with a group of leaders who were looking for ways to improve race relations in the city of Baltimore. Dr. Martin Jenkins, then president of Morgan State College, was a member of that group. He was a soft spoken, yet firm man, loved by the students and staff. I happened to discretely mention our plans to picket around City Hall on voting day, to inform the public about the meeting of the City Council. He didn't say much, as was his usual style.

When the day came, there were only about seven of us walking around the plaza in front of City Hall, including John White, Joseph Dixon, a few other community activists, and me. By late afternoon, a bus packed with black students from Morgan State College arrived with signs and joined the picket line. About five minutes after their arrival, a bus full of white students from Loyola College arrived with their signs. This was a paradigm of democracy at its best. I often wished I could have had a reunion with that group. I became so excited that since I was leading the line, I led them right into City Hall, up to the balcony. We raised our signs as the council looked on for about an hour. Subsequently, the bill passed with a vote of fourteen supporting it and seven against it.

Later, I met with Dr. Jenkins at his home, and he told me that the restructuring of the administration of colleges would not allow such impromptu actions in the future. He showed me some of the African artifacts he had found on his trip there, which left me wondering about visiting Africa myself.

We heard that Peter Angelos had returned to his law practice, after serving on the City Council. He went on to win several important class action suits against steel companies and finally purchased the Baltimore Orioles team.

About four years ago, I learned that a biography about the dynamic political figure, former Mayor William D. Schaefer, had been written by C. Fraser Smith. Out of admiration for the former politician and an interest in politics, I bought the book, hoping to find space in my home for one more piece of literature. For twelve years, I lived in the same district as he. In fact, our homes were one street and five blocks apart. I admired his hard work and support for equal rights, as well as other ideas he'd had for the city. Many times I drove down his block, thinking I might see him and tell him what a good job he was doing.

I read the book and noticed a statement about Peter Angelos unsuccessfully introducing the Public Accommodations Bill. In 2007, while my wife had a day off from teaching, we travelled to Baltimore to study the meeting records of the City Council regarding that bill. After spending the entire day making copies of the meeting notes, we could not find any negative positions by Mr. Angelos. The documents indicated that he was a strong supporter of the entire process of having that bill move through its three readings, and becoming an ordinance. He voted each time in favor of adding public accommodations to the original bill and changing the name of the agency to the Baltimore Human Rights Commission. Mr. Dixon introduced the final version of the bill that was signed into law by the mayor as Ordinance 1509 on June 8, 1962.

Except for that one bit of confusion, the book is one of the best and most thorough biographies I have read to date.

REFLECTIONS

In an attempt to examine our many struggles, John and I would frequently spend evenings meeting at one of our homes. We would strategize and discuss past and current events. As we reflected on the Civil Rights issue and our efforts to get the Public Accommodations Bill passed, we discussed the obstacles our people had to overcome. John talked about how he was raised in Meridian, Mississippi, and as a teenager, had gotten into a fight with a white teen. His parents quickly sent him to New York City to live with an aunt. He learned barbering skills, which meant he always had some money in his pocket, even during the Great Depression.

I led a successful campaign for John to secure a position in the Alliance district office, where he had become vice president. Simultaneously, he maintained the presidency of the local branch, and I was elected first vice president. When he took the other position, the members urged me to run, but I refused because I wanted to prove that performance is more important than a title, unless of course, it involved benefits. Being an organization composed primarily of minorities, and having the fewest number in each craft, except the mail handlers, it was ludicrous to campaign for a title when I could do almost anything I wanted to or had the time to accomplish in my position as first vice president.

I recently witnessed the chaos generated by such an attempt. During the state convention of a national organization, the first vice president sought the presidency. I had neither heard of him nor seen him anywhere. There was so much contention and chaos that the young college students we were trying to organize, walked out. It showed that this man felt it was more important to receive recognition than help maximize the efforts to improve the plight of our people.

In the Parliamentary Procedure class, I was taught that in a primarily volunteer community organization, there's enough work in any one position to keep one very busy, if the goal is to actually make a change in the community. At times it seems as if some don't mind fighting to see who is going to lead the fort. Education doesn't necessarily change the core self of a person.

I was determined to prove that blacks could work as a team, without regard for a title. In the Post Office, it was obvious how the local white officers had so much respect for each other that their members always appeared to be satisfied and loyal to the leaders they had elected. They seemed willing to work with and follow them, rather than sit back and criticize.

As soon as the Civil Rights movement began to have a little success, many small black organizations worked to do their own thing. After the passage of the Civil Rights Bill in 1964, those organizations dwindled. There was a failure to realize that assurance to maximize the effects of that bill demanded constant coordination and monitoring.

Just before Dr. Martin Luther King Jr. was assassinated, I heard several Civil Rights leaders mocking him, referring to him as "De Lord." When the news was reported that he had been shot and killed, those same leaders were saddened. I quietly observed the duplicity.

More than four decades later, things haven't changed much in that regard. We've finally elected a president of color. Yet, some of our black leaders seem determined to criticize and undermine his efforts to accomplish his agenda.

When a minority group views another minority group through the eyes of the oppressor, they become more vicious than the oppressor. We call that, "inverted chauvinism." As the saying goes, "Uncle Tom is in good health, and has never had a heart attack or cancer, but he sure needs one."

GRAND JURY AND DEPRESSION

Louise decided to apply for a job at the Post Office. She studied, easily passed the written test and scheme, and was immediately hired. Just as she'd begun working, Mrs. Tyler got sick.

We first noticed a couple of months prior that something was wrong when Louise's youngest sister, Jeanie, got married. After the wedding, Louise and I went back to Mrs. Tyler's house to pick up trays of food to bring to the reception hall, which was within walking distance. Mrs. Tyler was carrying a pan of ham. She walked down one step into her yard and fell face first, though she managed to keep the pan steady. She got right up, never said a word, and never missed another step. As time went on, she would occasionally black out and fall. Finally, she was taken to the hospital and diagnosed with a brain tumor. Louise became extremely depressed, yet continued to juggle work and take care of our girls.

As Mrs. Tyler's condition worsened, two or three days a week, after she got home from work, Louise would get the four girls and travel on three buses to visit her mother and cook and clean up after her. I would pick them up in the evening on my way home from work. Eventually, it was too much for Louise. So the postmaster secretly assigned her to light duty. When one of the white unions got wind of it, they complained to the point that she was required to return to full duty.

A little more than a year after her diagnosis, Mrs. Tyler died, leaving Louise absolutely devastated. She never fully recovered and could only find comfort in prescription anti-anxiety and anti-depressant pills. Needless to say, the demands of my work did little to help her.

In 1965, I was appointed to serve on the Baltimore City Grand Jury for three months. The duties were for the twenty-one of us, three of whom were black, to be sequestered to examine evidence of a particular case to determine if it was sufficient to present and indict. Sometimes there were photos and/or testimony from officers that, if presented for indictment, would be scheduled to go before a petit jury.

During the three-month period, we acted upon more than 2500 cases, averaging between forty and sixty per day. Almost three quarters of the cases concerned blacks involved in domestic violence, rape, robbery, and murder. These cases were flashing repeatedly before our eyes, all day long.

I became sympathetic toward the authorities who had to try to maintain objectivity, while working with the problems they faced. I could see the difference between the older and younger police officers. The younger ones would act rather raunchy, quick to make an arrest, while the more seasoned officers were wiser, engaging in a little more reasoning and discretion, not flaunting their authority.

After about a week of reviewing cases involving my own folk, I became overwhelmed and could hardly take anymore. I became friends with a black minister who was also on the jury. We often shared our frustrations about the critical condition of our people. One day he took me to a bar, which we continued to visit every day for lunch and a drink. This continued for about two weeks.

Gradually, we became a little more settled in the task and somewhat immune to the issues, and stopped drinking.

There was a policy that an undercover policeman could take us any place we wanted to visit. I made it a point to see everything I could. I was taken to black and white clubs, gay and lesbian after-hour joints, boys and girls detention schools, the Maryland Penitentiary, mental institutions, hospitals, and the morgue. It blew my mind in terms of the catastrophic destruction of the family structure.

For example, I visited a hospital that housed a section called the "snake pit." Most of the members of the grand jury chose not to visit. It was a large open room in the basement with a concrete floor. The patients looked about ten years old and older. The majority of them were white, and all of them were naked and deformed. A long urinal was built into the length of the wall for the males to use if they could. There were also several drains in the floor. I was informed that a hose was used to periodically wash the floor. These people were called "mongoloids," which we now understand to be Down Syndrome. Years ago, a mongoloid was described as one who was usually short in stature with narrow, slanted eyes, a flattened skull and mental deficiencies. In the midst of the horror, I realized that each of them was someone's child.

This experience helped me admire Uncle Thaddeus and Aunt Zulene Joyner, Mama's brother and his wife. The youngest of their children lived in a bassinet for twenty-two years. They carried him to the store, to church, and wherever else they went. They were devoted to him all his life, lovingly feeding him with a bottle, giving him pureed food, and keeping him warm and dry. Their ability to laugh and enjoy life, at the same time, was infectious.

When that tour of duty was over, I realized that I couldn't stay at the Post Office and work with satisfied, middle class black folks, who weren't going to do anything but go to work, get their money and return home. I couldn't handle being around people like that. I could no longer tolerate white folks who were discriminating, and black folks who unwilling to do anything about it. They would go to church and worship, but do nothing in the community. It got on my last nerve and became increasingly difficult for me to even go to work. When I did, I was often late and barely able to work eight hours.

I finally realized I was almost as miserable as my wife. Depression on both our parts continued to chisel away at the stability of our marriage and family. Louise's increased prescription drug use allowed her to cope as best she could. I massaged my way out by searching for more work.

A PRESCRIPTION FOR PROGRESS

March-ing. March-ing. March-ing. In cadence. Shouts. In sync. Two hundred strong.

The national Congress of Racial Equality (CORE) had come to town. I got excited. When I heard they were going to have a public meeting at the Baltimore Civic Center with leading city and state officials, I made it my business to be there.

During that meeting, it was declared that CORE had decided to pour a major portion of its resources and staff into Baltimore. It was to utilize those assets as its Target City Project to obtain equal rights and opportunities for all. At the time, a CORE branch had already been organized in Baltimore and was considered to be one of the most effective chapters in the country.

The Baltimore chapter had already initiated the Route 40 Program in 1962. Route 40 was the main thoroughfare between Washington and New York. Blacks could not eat in public places along that highway. CORE addressed this public accommodations issue when it initiated a direct action project to eliminate the practice.

Effective programs were also implemented in the areas of housing and public education. The housing program was mainly concerned with open occupancy in the city of Baltimore, and CORE encouraged the provision for better housing for blacks. This open occupancy program had the support of both black and white community groups. While there had been some administrative changes made in public schools, the system was still segregated.

CORE supported the efforts of the Teachers' Union to improve student education.

Baltimore, however, was considered by many to be a northern city, but struggled with many social problems typical of southern cities. An isolated atmosphere still lingered, in that blacks owned few businesses in their communities. Political disenfranchisement was also in place, and while no law prevented blacks from voting, many eligible voters were unregistered, and the number of elected black officials was few, compared to the estimated black population of more than forty percent.

Of all the things communicated at the meeting, I was struck by one major point. As part of the Target City Project, a Freedom School was being established to help the youth with their schoolwork and to take them to the library. Naturally, I immediately volunteered. Education, to me, was the path to permanent progress, as well as a positive way to break the trend of the lack of motivation to attend school and perform well. Based on my experience with the grand jury, I knew that chaos permeated in many inner city families and was not conducive to learning.

I volunteered to participate three nights a week by teaching math and English, and taking students to the library. I was one of two men from the city who made this commitment, along with about seven women from the national office. A few other women, also local staff members, taught at the school. The main focus of the national staff, however, was to help establish the school and then return home or report to another city.

To further expand the Target City Project, the national office committed most of its field staff to relocate to Baltimore in April 1966. The focus included voter registration drives and the development of a Maryland Freedom Union, a project to organize black employees in service occupations in businesses, such as hospitals and retail stores. It also aimed to develop government and privately funded programs to train and employ indigenous residents of Baltimore.

Three weeks into the program, the assistant director of the school informed me that they had submitted a proposal to the Department of Labor to provide the funds to train twenty-four men in Service Station Management. The age group was stipulated to range from eighteen to twenty-four. I was told that Humble Oil (now Exxon) would provide the service station and training for staff in all aspects of Service Station Management, including organization, financial accountability, and diagnostic procedures. It would be conducted at the Humble Retail Management School in Towson, Maryland. I was among a select few to attend the required six-week training classes for five days a week, six hours a day. Thereafter, at the assistant director's recommendation, I would direct the project.

I accepted the challenge, requested, and was granted an extended unpaid leave of absence from the Post Office for community service. The project was scheduled to begin December 1, 1966, with eight of us at the helm.

When training was over, CORE's Baltimore director, William Brown, said the proposal for funds had not been completed. The assistant director who recruited me to the position of director, had become ill and was hospitalized. He asked if I would revise the draft and submit it to the Office of Manpower, Policy Evaluation and Research (OMPER), a training arm of the United States Department of Labor. OMPER was established under the auspices of the Manpower Development Training Act. This project was to be under contract with OMPER for one year to determine if it would be successful enough to be refunded and expanded, or canceled.

Here I was, on leave without pay, to work on a project that barely existed. I had to rewrite the proposal three times.

The thrust to funding and continued support for the Target City Youth Program contained many lessons, surprises, and unexpected trials. Having been one of the few to receive a leave of absence, with no time restraint from the Post Office, and with much support from management, I was quite determined to achieve success. I was, after all, a black man who had scored the highest grade of any other black on the Supervisor's exam in the Baltimore City Post Office; yet, I still had to prove to myself that I was credible. My intention was to represent my race and the Post Office, which had a good reputation regarding the performance of its employees.

FACING BUREAUCRACY

When I began meeting with Director Gilmore of OMPER, who was black, he assigned me to his white deputy to weigh the merits of the proposal. The deputy director didn't support the project because its ultimate written objective was to train the men to become managers. He gave me quite a hard time.

I honestly felt the goal of training anyone to become qualified to manage a service station in a short period of time was unrealistic. I had bought my first old car when I was seventeen years old, before I entered the military. After I was discharged, before even thinking about the Target City Youth Program, I had bought seven more, and only one was new. With a family and limited income, I had to learn how to maintain each car myself, if I expected to travel.

The main resource for service station operation during that era came from repairing automobiles and selling parts, and I knew those skills required immense study, training, discipline, and financial accountability.

I strongly believed, however, that if we could just get our feet in the door, we could make a difference and motivate some of the inner city youth to get off the corners, go back to school, or at least become productive and independent adults. That became the main objective of the staff. At least the battle to develop a constructive adult could be won without the shedding of blood.

Director Gilmore, however, had faith in the project, and we were given conditional approval for a grant of $144,000 for one year. If successful, it would receive additional funding. The staff would consist of eight people; a director, to which I was appointed, a secretary, three team leaders, one counselor, and two academic instructors.

I also faced the last-minute requirement of raising $5,000 seed money. Naturally, when people in the poor community try to make a change in their lives for the better, resources become scarce. I was panicky, but optimistic. I prayed a lot and believed that God did not bring me this far to leave me. I traveled to Washington several times to raise the funds, though I had only enough money for gas and parking. It seemed like I would not be able to get started.

Finally, Director Gilmore referred William Brown and me to an official in the Office of Economic Opportunity. We explained our dilemma. He sent for a staff attorney so that we could reiterate that plight to him. He requested that the attorney find out what could be done to get us the $5,000. After a long pause, the attorney concluded that he could not find any regulation to cover us, but offered a list of policies that would make it impossible for us to receive a contribution.

I will never forget the official's response. "I did not ask you what we can't do. I want you to find a legal way by which we *can* do something."

The attorney left while we continued planning. About an hour later, he returned with a "quid pro quo" regarding how the department could offer legal assistance. The department would have to buy something from us that would benefit them.

We were given a project to perform. Two days later, after working twelve hours each day, we completed the assignment. I returned to the Office of Economic Opportunity and placed a detailed thesis on Education and Community Development on his desk. Since he was a visionary with a deep understanding of the need for community progression and achievement, we received the funds.

TARGET CITY YOUTH PROGRAM

Target City Youth Program was ready to begin. But before we could solicit any young trainees, William Brown advised me that the staff would be required to attend a sensitivity session one day for about six hours to determine our commitment and loyalty. The Civil Rights Movement had attracted many people with ulterior motives. It was also intended to develop a sense of pride in what we were doing.

Brown conducted the session, without breaks. Once it was complete, I believed we had a dedicated and competent team. After we had been in operation for about three months, however, we were informed that we would have to participate in a more comprehensive and stressful sensitivity session scheduled for a weekend in a motel, including members of the national staff, local chapter members of CORE, and the Target City staff. There were about twenty of us enrolled.

The session was conducted by two black psychologists. Again, this session was supposedly designed to determine one's sense of confidence, dedication, and loyalty to the cause and methodology of CORE. It was very grueling. Sessions lasted eight continuous hours the first day, twelve hours the second day, and a two-hour review the third day.

By the end of the first six hours, two ladies expressed having a crush on me, which completely surprised me. Then one of the staff members I had hired became hostile and emotionally out of control. He admitted he was not qualified for the position and resigned the following day. I had to rush and hire a replacement.

A white man on the national staff, who was exceptionally friendly, left as well, allegedly because he was exposed as having another purpose for volunteering to be on the national staff, besides engaging in a relationship with one of the black female members. A few days later, he left Baltimore.

At its conclusion, it was evaluated that some participants needed additional training, but that I had been an effective leader. However, the most serious crisis occurred about two weeks later.

When we were ready for students, the team leaders and I went door to door to solicit trainees for enrollment in Target City. The facility was located in the heart of the poorest of the poor section of Baltimore City, and we had to overcome the attitude of the young men who preferred standing on the corner doing nothing but killing time and protecting their turf.

A major factor in our recruitment process was that the students would receive a stipend of $20 per week for participating in the project. We knew we couldn't refuse the opportunity to anyone because it would give the impression that we were only concerned with making ourselves seem successful by enrolling those who already had the desire to improve their lives.

The initial class consisted of twenty-four students, two of whom were illiterate, and fifteen who had already been arrested for minor crimes. The average level of education was third grade.

Our first assignment was to supervise and train three teams of eight trainees each in the service station operation. Also, each team was scheduled for academic instruction in reading, writing, and arithmetic. Each team leader had a rotating shift which included working the afternoon shift and closing the station nightly at eleven o'clock.

One evening, after most had gone home, the Baltimore director, and my immediate supervisor, called me to have a conference in his office. I was informed that one of my team leaders was teaching his team target practice with his pistol in the station during the evening shift, and it had to stop before the public complained and we lost our funding. The director also confessed that he was having an affair with the team leader's wife.

Here I am with a dysfunctional team leader and a womanizing superior, and everyone living in proximity to each other, except me. I waited a couple of days before acting, when I would have plenty of time, and when the team leader had rotated to the day shift and appeared to be relaxed. I waited until all my staff, except those across the street in the service station and their trainees, had gone home. The team leader remained on duty. I made an appointment with him to meet me in my office after I had finished some necessary paperwork.

For about eight hours, I met with the team leader, trying to get a better understanding of his personality and stress level. In closing, he wrote me a memo of resignation, effective immediately. He said he knew the national director would transfer him to another city.

Two days later, all the students demanded a meeting with me and my staff because the team leader told them I had fired him. They were as hostile as ever. I read them his letter of resignation, but either they could not or would not understand the difference between resignation and termination. We were in our largest classroom while my staff, William Brown, and my supervisor sat beside me. After about a half hour of my explaining the gist of the meeting, without releasing the entire confidential conversation, I informed them that I stood by my decision to allow him to resign.

The trainees began yelling and screaming threats that they were going to blow the place up. Since I realized long ago where I was working, I was never "naked." I didn't expose myself and, therefore, wasn't too concerned. When they stormed out, my supervisor gave me a piece of advice as he was leaving: "Never box a rat in a corner with no way out. That's bad strategy."

I felt that I was in charge of the trainees, and unacceptable behavior could not be tolerated for the sake of peace. I asked my staff members to locate the trainees. I figured they would be out and about in the neighborhood. A short time later, the staff returned, reporting that some were hanging out in the pool hall, while others were on a corner near a restaurant. I told them to find the young guys at the pool hall and shoot pool with them, while other staff members took the rest of the trainees to a restaurant and bought them something to eat. Their stipend arrived the next day, but I withheld their checks until they returned to the project.

The accused team leader in question was transferred to another state in the Midwest. After the national CORE office fired William Brown a year later, the former team leader was brought back to Baltimore as my director. It took another year for the national office to realize its error, which was that the man had minimal managerial skills. He was removed, leaving me in charge of the project without local supervision.

From that point forward, we began paying more attention to the trainees in other ways besides service station maintenance. Time was taken out to play contact sports, such as football and boxing, a surprise to some of them. It was quite revealing that those who seemed very shy and silent in the classroom were physically adept, as opposed to those who were loquacious and cocky. Sports had become an equalizer.

ACCOUNTABILITY

What I didn't realize was that the service station operation required a special system for accounting, which had to be reconciled twice daily. The funded project stipulated that the secretary was responsible for coordinating and reconciling the grant funds, correspondence, and coordinating student records. But I had hired an accountant part-time to reconcile the financial records of the service station. That was before computers. All we had were typewriters and mimeograph machines.

Since I worked ten to twelve hours a day, at least six, sometimes seven days a week, I would simply store every receipt in a drawer with the intent of organizing them at the end of the fiscal year.

One day, just before the end of the contract, I received a call from an auditor from Washington, notifying me that he would be in my office in ten minutes to audit my records. I felt trapped. When he arrived, I showed him my drawer full of receipts, and he just walked out, saying there was nothing he could do, and would call me later. Meanwhile, there wasn't much money left in the budget to pay normal expenses, such as staff, rent, utilities, etc.

I realized I needed to be the one to organize and prepare the report for audit. I believed that to manage, I had to know the details of expenditures of the grant. Other programs in Baltimore were being closed because of failure to pass an audit by the funding agency. I had never experienced a professional audit and didn't know what to expect. When I began organizing the receipts,

I realized it would be a time-consuming venture. I was afraid of losing staff because the one-year contract was over, and all the funds were spent as allocated in the contract.

I happened to participate with the national CORE on a picket line in Washington, D.C. to demand that the Department of Labor, among other issues, provide more funding for similar programs around the country. About 150 of us participated in the march. We walked in a wide circle in front of the Labor building without signs. As we filed into the building, we noticed a long line of policemen in riot gear standing at attention along a nearby alley wall. We then assembled in the auditorium where James Farmer, the founder and original director of CORE, gave an eloquent speech.

Someone then decided that a select group of us should go to the office of William Wirtz, secretary of Labor, with our concerns. About twenty of us gathered in the office on a Friday. After the discussion came to a stalemate, some began talking about the possibility of a weekend sit-in in the office.

Among us, stood a white observer. I quietly asked him whom I could see about procuring emergency funds for my project. He referred me to a nearby office. I immediately slipped out and went to an official who didn't even have a name plate on his door. His name was Mr. McConnell, director of Operations, who suggested I write out the amount of funds needed for each line item for the estimated five weeks I needed to prepare the audit.

I wrote the items out quickly: rent, supplies, salaries, utilities, etc. Then I followed him to another operation. He didn't give an order. He sat down, handed a clerk an invoice, along with my handwritten budget, and asked her, "Would you mind doing me a favor? Can you see to it that a check for this amount be mailed out this afternoon so Mr. Holmes can receive it by tomorrow?"

I truly appreciated his style – gracious yet professional with his support staff. I had seen enough superiors barking at support staff, which I didn't find appropriate. I received the check the next day.

I had an accountant whose duties were to reconcile the records of the service station operation. He was employed full time at a Baltimore college. After categorizing the receipts correctly, along with a corresponding voucher, he recommended we hire a young CPA who had more experience in grants, and knew a system for monitoring a business on a regular basis.

Pete Engleman demonstrated a simple accounting system to illustrate the financial status of the organization quickly, and prepare us for the audit. Eventually, I incorporated the system in each contract I was ever involved in after that, including the churches I would pastor. I am still grateful for the knowledge because I have never had another problem with an audit.

THE FIRST GRADUATING CLASS

About six months after the project began, the training was complete, and it was time for the trainees to graduate. We prepared a commencement program and invited their families and friends to attend. The trainees were instructed to wear a jacket, shirt, and tie, so we could take pictures.

When the graduation was set to begin, everyone showed up but the trainees. I sent the staff to look for them, and they were found on different corners. The young men didn't want to participate in the ceremony because none of them owned or had ever worn a suit or tie. It was something we had taken for granted, and we were disappointed that this issue had never been addressed.

We got them neckties, taught them how to tie them, and held that brief ceremony on the Target City premises in the large classroom on the ground floor of the school. Some even wore African turbans. Songs were sung, speeches were given, and the proud young men were handed certificates. We took pictures and enjoyed the refreshments.

Subsequently, there was never an issue with recruitment and the training process. We always had a waiting list to enroll. The lessons we learned the first year enabled us to have a stronger footing as we moved forward to proposing and developing our next phase.

EXPANDING THE PROJECT

Target City Youth Program had exceeded expectations, opinions, and demands of the public and government. I wanted to broaden the project; so with our next proposal, we prepared and submitted our request for $444,000, to include an additional service station and a secretarial school. Unfortunately, we encountered another road block. The United States Department of Labor demanded the funding be monitored by the State of Maryland.

CORE's national director, Floyd McKissick, made an appointment with the secretary of the Department of Labor to protest that reassignment. We recognized that most projects initiated by blacks that went through the State were soon discontinued for one reason or another. The commissioner agreed, and a meeting was arranged for me to meet at the Department of Labor with Mr. McConnell and a representative from the Department of Health, Education and Welfare (HEW) to transfer the proposal from the Labor Department to HEW.

It was the winter of 1968. In the snow, I made a trip to Washington, D. C. to meet with the officials. When I arrived, the HEW official turned the proposal over and sarcastically said he wasn't going to deal with it because he didn't have time to read it. Here he was, not far from his building, and I had driven forty miles in a snow storm, only to be told he didn't have time to read it.

I blew up and blasted him with every sarcastic phrase I could think of. Anytime I experienced blatant arrogance on a personal level, it was difficult for me not to explode because of my lifelong experience with bias, including the plight of the Tuskegee Airmen who had fought overseas. My classmates and I admitted that we had become bitter and rebellious. We believed we were living in a foreign land and wondered how we would respond as civilians. By now, my patience and tolerance levels were short. I stormed out of the office and went directly to Vice President Hubert Humphrey's office. The snow had fallen almost six inches by then. The administrative assistant was in the office, but the vice president was out of town. I explained my dilemma to him, who said he would see what he could do.

Initially, I preferred to take the grievance to one of the three congressmen, Messrs. George Fallon, Samuel Friedel, or Edward Garmatz. I also considered Senator Daniel Brewster or Senator Joseph Tydings. However, since they lived in Baltimore, Maryland, which was only forty miles from Washington, D. C., I knew they would be sleep at that late hour. When I was working in the Post Office, our labor union, the National Alliance, always invited them to our banquets. We knew the value and success of first voting for, and then supporting the politicians we elected.

That evening, when I returned home, the vice president's administrative assistant called and told me to contact the HEW official and apologize for my callous remarks. So, I did, and I could almost hear him smiling on the phone. He told me to contact him in a couple of days, and he would have a date for signing the approval of the proposal.

The day of signing for the grant was agreed upon. I invited Mr. Perot, a member of the CORE national staff to come from New York and accompany us to the signing. He had originally selected me to direct Target City and was unable to complete the first proposal because he was hospitalized. Two of my staff members, Roy Moody and Frank Pullen, accompanied me to witness the signing so they would have a feel for the process and share a token recognition for the great work they had done. After all, I reasoned, without their dedication, discipline, and skills, there would not have been a second chance.

The scheduled signing time was eleven o'clock in the morning, which meant we left Baltimore around nine o'clock, while Mr. Perot had to leave New York by six o'clock. When we arrived, the HEW official claimed to have about eight proposals stacked on his desk awaiting review. Since six of them happened to be on top of ours, he said he may not get to our approval by the end of the day.

I was tired, tense, embarrassed, and irate. I hollered up and down that hall until most of the personnel came out of their office to see this mad dog. I finally got sense enough to go to the office of the official who had originally approved the project and anxiously informed him of the treatment I had experienced from his staff members. He requested I return that afternoon.

Meanwhile, I was also furious because of the inconvenience to Mr. Perot. Roy and Frank whispered to me that Mr. Perot seemed disgusted and had gone across the street to a restaurant for breakfast. They reminded me how insecure he was, and that I should apologize to him for the unexpected response, to which I obliged. He didn't comment on the neglect and unfairness of the official, or about his own inconvenience. He just cussed me out for wearing a tiny pin on my jacket labeled "NAPE," the acronym for the National Alliance of Postal Employees, the former labor union to which I had belonged and had been responsible for what I had achieved.

I don't remember how long it was, but for a considerable amount of time, I wished that murder was legal because Perot and the HEW official would have breathed their last breath that day. After finishing breakfast, he drove back to New York without participating in the proposal signing.

When we returned later that afternoon, the HEW official was not in the office. We signed for the grant with another official. I was informed that the previous official had received his transfer orders to another state.

A year or so later, I was teased by a couple of officials from HEW about how I had grown beyond my militant stance to a more sophisticated, yet still determined, style.

The HEW official later told me that he used that same sarcastic and nonchalant technique on the national office of CORE to determine its level of professionalism. According to him, the result was not favorable.

Based on our experience with the various attitudes and styles of the national office of CORE, we felt their strategy would encourage violence and threats, rather than negotiating and reasoning. After all, we knew every other CORE chapter had been closed under this political administration, and by allegedly peaceful means. We were one of the last ones standing.

I considered the approval and signing for the grant a second time, along with an increase from $144,000 for the first grant to $444,000, a major accomplishment.

SELF-IMPROVEMENT

As excited as I was about Target City's success in renewing our contract for $444,000, I realized I was reaching the Peter Principle: "Every person in an organization tends to rise to his or her level of incompetence."

I needed some help, a right hand man. So I went to my old friend and union leader in the Post Office, Joe Dixon, director of Welfare. Fortunately, because of our successful first year, he was able to get a leave of absence to serve as my deputy.

As a two-man team, we took a two-week course in Executive Decision Making. I had taken about eight courses while working at the Post Office, but now I needed more. We also enrolled in courses with Dale Carnegie, including Public Speaking and Executive Development. I even served as an assistant after taking each course, and required that some of my staff take some courses as well.

Joe and I met a highly skilled black psychologist, Harts Brown, who gave us a series of tests and prescribed some courses for us to take at the Baltimore Social Security Building, as part of a master's program at George Washington University. Though difficult, the courses were helpful. One course addressed the pros and cons of the computer. I, of course, approved of this new baby for the sake of communication, even though it was a very new tool.

I was also ready for another facility to house a secretarial training school. Since banks were unsympathetic to blacks, I appealed to Little Willie, an astute black businessman, who assisted many of our people in buying property and owning their own businesses. Many of us Baltimoreans believed he was really a racketeer, but we didn't care. When we were in a bind to get loans, we went to him. He would readily loan the money with interest, of course, and a reasonable period of time to pay it off. He was very soft-spoken and approachable. When I told him what I needed the loan for, I got it. I was able to secure another small building, until enrollment increased, requiring an additional larger building.

I believe it was the Cardinal Archdiocese of the Baltimore Catholic Church, who donated a school building for a nominal fee of one dollar per year for more classrooms to be used for academics. This helped boost the enrollment of young women. We now had all the resources needed to instruct them in clerical skills and help them prepare for the Civil Service exam, and government employment.

Another service station with four bays was leased to us by the Humble Oil Company, agreeing to convert one bay into a classroom to make room for more trainees at Target City.

I needed someone to operate the second station and assist in the training of its future auto mechanics. I made my choice and informed the Humble Oil executives. They said he would have to take the written exam on Service Station Management to qualify. I, along with my original staff members, had passed the exam and had been informed that I had gotten the highest score. The person I had chosen to manage the new operation took the exam and failed. I accused them of racial bias for requiring blacks to take the exam. After a great deal of persuasion, they reluctantly agreed to hire Haywood Bryant, who successfully managed that station for more than fifteen years. We became a good team.

When the original six of us attended Humble Retail Management School in 1966, the emphasis was on automobile repair, sale of supplies, and diagnosis. We had to fill out a hypothetical form on Fridays, stating how much we had sold in materials, oil, and gasoline versus automobile diagnosis and repair.

One team emphasized gas sales and other items like oil and antifreeze. They concluded that the fast service of gasoline was the strong emphasis. Surprisingly, that team had a higher profit than most other teams. I could foresee a change coming to replace the dual purpose service station. I believed strongly that auto service would become specialized with fast service for gasoline, and separate facilities for repair and supplies, because of the training required for auto repair and maintenance.

1968

The year, 1968, was an exceptional time for Civil Rights, packed with accomplishments. Robert Kennedy, who continued the legacy of his brother, President John Kennedy, a champion of minorities' rights, had claimed victory in the California primary and had enough delegates to win the Democratic nomination for president.

Carl Stokes became the first black mayor of Cleveland, a major American city in Ohio. One of the most outstanding events that brought an enormous amount of pride and emotion occurred in October. Two black sprinters, Tommy Smith and John Carlos, ran the 200-meter race in the Olympics in Mexico City, Mexico, coming in first and third. At the gold medal ceremony, while the Star Spangled Banner played, they each raised a black-gloved fist in the air, representing the cry for freedom and an approval of the Civil Rights struggle.

Contrarily, we also fell into a state of deep devastation and grief when Dr. Martin Luther King Jr. was assassinated in April, and when Robert Kennedy was assassinated in June. The loss of Dr. King caused outbursts of riots and destruction in Baltimore. Our building was situated in the center of the indigent urban section of East Baltimore. My office was located on the second floor, which was used as a multi-purpose facility for classrooms, meetings, equipment storage, and supplies. The headquarters for the CORE staff was across the street next to the service station used for training. I could look out my window at all the destruction around us. Fortunately, our buildings had not been touched, nor was a market on the same block that sold quality groceries for reasonable prices.

Our training continued in the midst of that rebellion. On the Saturday after Dr. King had been killed, I received a call that a few of my staff members, along with some of the community leaders, wanted to meet in my building that night to determine our strategy. When I arrived, about twelve of them were sitting in the dark room on the floor against the four walls. As some began talking about getting involved in rioting, I quickly glanced around the room to determine if I knew everyone.

I spotted a young black stranger, someone I had never seen before. Some instigated about shooting the first white man they saw. Others suggested burning a few buildings, and so on. I never said a word, and neither did the stranger. At the end of the meeting, he approached me.

"Holmes, may I ride with you so I can get home?"

I consented. There was little conversation during the ride. Finally, he asked a simple question. "Holmes, what are you going to do?"

"Nothing," I replied out of suspicion, "but if you want to do anything, do something that would affect the masses – except killing."

When I arrived at his drop-off point, he thanked me for the ride, got out and started walking. I never saw where he ended up.

"This is a dubious character," I said to myself as I drove off.

Soon the riots heated to such a boiling point that a curfew was issued. No one could be on the street past four o'clock without permission from the authorities. Violation of the curfew meant an automatic arrest and at least twenty-four hours in jail.

A couple of days later, I saw the stranger on the street being arrested after curfew. Early the next morning, I happened to look out my office window and there he was, walking down the street. I wondered how he had been released from jail so quickly.

About three years later, I read a newspaper article about an organized student rebellion at a predominately black college. The same stranger was mentioned as the leader of the Baltimore protest.

Ah ha! I said to myself.

I would meet this stranger again years later when I worked as an Equal Employment Opportunity investigator and later became a supervisor. One of the investigators, a white woman, told me she couldn't find a particular company guilty of an obvious violation of the law, because she lived in the area, and her taxes would increase. She had already demonstrated to me a certain lack of dedication. The staff of six to which I was assigned, worked in offices that were equally located on both sides of a narrow hallway that was around six feet long. The practice was that only if one had a client could the door be closed, and if not, it would remain open. All the work done was supposed to be extremely confidential, and because of our record-keeping, I always knew when there would be a visitation.

One day, the same woman had her office door closed. Since there was no record of a scheduled client, she was violating the unwritten "open-door" policy. I opened her door to find her lying on the floor with her legs stretched up the wall, and the same young stranger in the same position on the opposite wall.

Ah ha! I said to myself again. I had startled them, and invited him to leave immediately.

Naturally, I wondered what all of this meant in terms of the effectiveness of the EEOC, an agency that existed for the purpose of improving the relationships of everyone in a confidential manner. I reported what I had seen to my superior. I concluded that it is relatively easy for an official to decrease the efficacy of an organization after a short period of time. I didn't see her again. Nothing more was ever said about it and I didn't ask. All I know is that one day she was gone without a word.

TRAINEE DEVELOPMENT

One of the lessons we learned from the first training class in Target City was the importance of changing strategies to include exposure to different activities, thereby, further developing the trainees' social skills. We discussed that none of the trainees had either been to a bank or traveled outside of East Baltimore. To broaden the experience of this new group, we rotated them to participate in depositing funds with the team leader into bank accounts that we had established.

We also integrated other social activities besides contact sports, including trips to the beach, the park, and restaurants. They were taken on a bus trip to Luray Caverns in Virginia and to New York City to have lunch with CORE's national director, Mr. McKissick. The trainees presented him with a gift to demonstrate appropriate respect for a superior. Thereafter, socializing and appropriate public behavior was rarely an issue, and the trainees and the staff created a cohesive bond of teamwork. These were principles that I had learned from my father, had been reinforced at Tuskegee, and proved instrumental in the success of the Target City Youth Program. In other words, it was deemed important to broaden their knowledge of various environments beyond their immediate communities, and to meet and associate with people more educated than they. They had to realize life as a continuing growth process, and believe that they could advance their own positions.

At the end of the second class, the staff remembered some of the problems faced with the first class and decided to become more involved with the students. We did not assume they knew how to dress for graduation. We wanted them to have input and participation in the planning of their graduation.

As the big day approached, the trainees were persuaded to purchase dashikis. This time the graduation ceremony was held at Dunbar High School, where I had graduated twenty-five years earlier. Some of the graduates were encouraged to speak, and all were given the opportunity to participate in some way. Certificates were presented, and pictures were taken. We all had a more rewarding experience this time around and came to the conclusion that we had to anticipate potential problems and not take anything for granted.

PROJECT EXPANSION

Target City Youth Program continued to flourish. At its inception, we were awarded $144,000 for the first year and $444,000 for the following year. Now we were trying to secure approval for a $1 million grant.

The fiasco with Mr. Perot from the national office of CORE for the second grant was instrumental in my decision to have the attorney who represented that office, Mr. Josephson, assist us in procuring this important new grant. We scheduled an appointment to meet him for lunch at a prominent place in New York City.

Joe Dixon, Frank Pullen, and I left Baltimore about five minutes later than I had wanted to. I was determined to be on time. When I drove past Exit 3 on the New Jersey Turnpike, I increased my speed to eighty miles per hour. By the time I passed Exit 4, I was driving ninety miles per hour. A state trooper stationed on the side of the road pulled me over and began writing me a speeding ticket. I begged him to please hurry up with the ticket because I was going to a meeting on Wall Street to negotiate a million-dollar contract. He smiled, handed me the ticket, and I sped off doing ninety-five miles per hour.

We arrived about five minutes early. Frank had forgotten to wear a suit jacket and had to borrow one before entering the dining room. We explained to Mr. Josephson our objective. He agreed to meet us the day of the signing and arrived before we did. He whispered that he would show me how to operate. He told me a certain high-level official who was campaigning for election to a position of influence, would be calling him exactly one half hour after the meeting began. He would call on the agency phone in the office where the signing was held, thereby impressing the attendees.

When the phone rang, the secretary on the other end said excitedly, "Sergeant Shriver would like to speak with you."

Mr. Josephson picked up the phone and had a brief conversation, while getting the reaction he had anticipated. We were all so impressed that he had rubbed shoulders with a member of the Kennedy family. We signed for the $1 million grant soon thereafter.

We continued to grow and expand, increasing the number of staff members from twenty-one to thirty-five. We also included a printing shop and received $500,000 worth of printing equipment. Procuring printing machines required some unusual support and research regarding who had the most influence in the area in that regard. I learned that Maryland Congressman Samuel Friedel was a member of the Joint Printing Committee of Congress. He had frequently attended the functions we sponsored in the Postal Alliance, along with other elected officials, and I had met with him several times before regarding other issues. This time, as in the past, I made an appointment with him through his administrative assistant, Miss Justice, who was always courteous and ensured that our meetings were held in a timely fashion. We would periodically send her a "thank-you" card. Through Congressman Friedel, we got our printing equipment.

The Social Security Administration allowed some of its staff to take a leave of absence in order to teach the students how to develop printing skills and operate the machinery. In those days, there was only one large black-owned printing business in

Baltimore, and we saw an opportunity for expansion of small businesses in that area.

Additionally, we established a relationship with a married couple who owned a ceramics factory and created their own signature paints, molds, and equipment to produce unique ceramic artifacts, especially pieces that were African-inspired. They offered five of us a complimentary course in learning the craft. We readily accepted, seeing it as an opportunity to become knowledgeable in a profession that had barely been accessible to blacks before then. We also had a vision to establish a rehabilitation program using ceramic-making as therapy for seniors and those with disabilities and/or injuries.

As a result, they donated one kiln, and I bought two more. Through our famous chief benefactor, Little Willie, I was able to use some of his resources to procure another building for the rehab program.

Baltimore City had promised a grant to invest in a halfway house near the downtown area to establish a re-entry program for people who had been released from jail. We also had temporary approval to build ninety-eight units of housing in East Baltimore. To incorporate these other ventures, a corporation was formed in the name of Target City Youth Program. Since we had been involved with self-development for my staff and me, I required that we take more public speaking workshops with the Dale Carnegie Program.

Then we had trouble.

When I became director of Target City Youth Program, I began under the auspices of Floyd McKissick, a lawyer who was the second national director of CORE, succeeding James Farmer, its founder. McKissick was very supportive. During that time, CORE's focus was to fight racism with non-violence and support the principles of Dr. Martin Luther King Jr. There were hundreds of whites who joined our struggles and supported our beliefs.

Target City and other projects fashioned during those turbulent times depended on whites for their initial and continued existence. Target City, in particular, depended on whites for funding as well. We depended on them for the donation of a service station and a school, as well as for the purchase of $500,000 worth of printing equipment to train our youth to work in the printing business. And since there was only one black printing business in Baltimore at the time, we depended on a few white printing businesses to accept some of our trainees. The Social Security Administration allowed our trainees to receive additional training on their equipment. Whites also agreed to provide ceramics training.

Whites contributed generous funds for the Civil Rights Movement and participated in the Freedom Rides during the 1960s to fight discrimination against blacks. In a strategic move, some had agreed to ride in the back of the bus, while blacks rode in the front. They would refuse to move, even when ordered. At bus stops, they would go into the waiting room designated for coloreds, and blacks went into the waiting room designated for whites, using all the facilities, refusing to leave. This plan of action was designated to motivate the racists of the South to create a disastrous situation, so that the federal government would be coerced to enforce the law. Not only did blacks lose their lives, but so did many of our white allies and supporters.

CORE was supposed to be vigilant at enforcing the Civil Rights Act of 1964, which prohibited discrimination based on race, color, sex, religion, or national origin. For reasons unknown to me,

CORE's policies became more radical, its constitution was amended to prohibit any white members, but to allow them to be friends of CORE only.

Target City's primary goal was to be a model for the implantation of the Civil Rights Act. Instead of being a model for community accord, we were now practicing reverse discrimination. Although I was not aware of any whites applying for membership, it was difficult for the staff and me to acquiesce to this new policy. In other words, to us, civil rights also meant the right to organize and develop effective leadership, which encompasses two major roles. One was to fight discrimination as effectively as possible, and the other was to be a model for accepting those who were different. In particular, this included the poor, immigrants, members of other faiths, and different races. In fact, except for the Native Americans, we are all immigrants through our ancestors.

We had a personal experience in the Post Office regarding the sacrifices some whites had endured on behalf of integration. After the Freedom Rides began in the South, a white postal employee in Baltimore, William Moore, wanted to participate. In order to do it legitimately, he joined our union, the Baltimore branch of the National Alliance of Postal Employees, and applied for a leave of absence to join the Freedom Rides.

Moore decided on a symbolic walk from Baltimore to the South. Word quickly came back that he was shot point blank in the head in a southern state. I attended the interracial memorial service held in a church in downtown Baltimore.

CORE LEADERSHIP

When Roy Innis became the new director of CORE, the organization took a more radical and cancerous approach to the Civil Rights cause. The staff at Target City was required to participate in military-style boot camps, which incorporated more self-defense and war-time techniques. We were required to march through parks and other wooded areas, obeying certain military commands, and performing actual war-simulated tactics. We spent nights outdoors with little self-care facilities and scarce food. Some men and women employees slept in the back of pick-up trucks crammed together like sardines, while others slept on the ground on thin covers.

Target City made a more stringent attempt to pull away from this brute force instruction and retain the values and principles from which it was conceived. We believed in being that example of how to achieve racial harmony through education and cooperation. The first step to this goal was to improve the lives of young adults in order to motivate succeeding generations. The more intense our program became, the more resistance we met from CORE. Anonymous telephone threats were railed against me, my staff, and my family. My staff and I had concrete reason to believe that CORE's intent was to take over the project by force and destroy it. We began preparing ourselves for an inevitable attack from them, arming ourselves for protection, and assigning a couple of staff members to watch over my family.

Meanwhile, HEW called and warned me that they wouldn't fund my program unless I broke with CORE, since Target City was under the auspices of CORE. A short time later, we wrote bylaws and established our corporation with the state in order to separate ourselves from CORE. The entire staff met and approved the corporation so that the program could retain its integrity of racial integration, as opposed to racial segregation that CORE spearheaded. We also knew that all the other chapters in the country had been closed for one reason or another. Initially, CORE had sponsored an annual African American Christmas card sale with ethnic designs that were quite popular. It was reported that the average amount of funds raised was $60,000 to $75,000 annually. This project was suddenly discontinued without explanation.

With the tension increasing, I recognized that our phones were probably being tapped. I remember engaging in a conversation, and when it ended, I was inadvertently hesitant in hanging up my phone, and heard a click before I had completely hung up. From then on, I made it a point to always be careful of what I said on the phone; yet I wouldn't hang up until I heard that "click." I said to myself, "You can run, but you can't hide." I believed that someone was either trying to protect me or we had a mole in the organization.

Finally, I received a call from CORE leaders. They were coming to town to meet with us. We knew it would be a physical confrontation. Therefore, my staff advised me to stay home and coordinate from there. I assigned Joe, my dependable deputy, to attend on my behalf. About an hour before the meeting, Joe called and said his wife had received a threat and he would have to remain at home. I told him that if he was not at the meeting, all would be lost. We would lose Target City. I knew the staff was loyal to me, but many of them didn't have the discipline to stay organized in a crisis situation. He insisted on staying home. I knew it was all over.

Later, I was told that CORE had at least two automobiles packed with thugs, who after dark, would drive in front of our office building, stop, and pound the horn. Then they'd drive away. A few minutes later, they would return, blow the horn again and drive off. This would happen over and over again until staff members who were protecting the building finally ran out, jumped in their cars and chased them in an attempt to overtake them. It was CORE's strategy to lure our staff out of the building. Roy Innis arranged for a couple of other cars occupied with his men to be parked across the street. Once the Target City cars were out of sight, the other men, led by Innis and Waverly Yates, one of CORE's staff members allegedly from Connecticut, jumped out of their cars, ran in, and took over the facilities. I was told they hid their weapons in the panels that covered the lights in the ceiling. The police were called but, when they arrived, found nothing.

A few days later, Innis insisted I meet with him again. This time I agreed. Even though I felt like I was being thrust into a quagmire, I wanted to get a feel for the dynamics between us.

"Milton," Innis pressed, a hint of Virgin Island accent present, "you're bigger in Baltimore than I am in the whole country, and I can't have that. See, now, I believe in Machiavelli. You got thirty-five staff members. I've got four or five. I can't have that. Come with me and they'll fund me."

"I'll think about it," was all I could muster, and left.

I was familiar with Niccolo Machiavelli, a fifteenth century humanist and writer, whose approach to leadership was based on his theory that a new leader must stabilize his power at all costs, even if it means immorality and corruption, while exacting lies, deceit and brute force.

HEW contacted me and said they would no longer fund Target City. They would, however, fund CORE for an additional year. I knew it was a political decision. After considering all the factors and discussing the issues with the staff, I was convinced of my position.

Without notice, I went to Innis' hotel room to give him my answer face-to-face. When I walked in, I was shocked to see Joe Dixon, my loyal deputy and friend, sitting there. Piecing the puzzle together, I sat down. Joe never said a word. After a few moments of tense conversation, I was asked again.

"Come with us. We'll get funding."

I stood up and said, "I'm not going to work with you," and left.

James Farmer, at the time, worked for President Richard Nixon as deputy assistant secretary for administration in HEW. We believed his was a powerless position because it was said that he had no authority over finances. Farmer eventually left, so I appealed to him, and he committed to support us.

Innis, I discovered later, had allegedly gone to Farmer and convinced him that if he supported Target City, CORE would be dead, and CORE was the organization he had founded.

So the rumor came back that since Farmer was in the process of retiring, Nixon asked if he wanted anything. Farmer desired nothing but to save CORE. He also required that I work with Innis. I knew that would never happen.

Target City was then accused of withholding its financial and training records from the past four years from CORE. Charges were filed in court, and Target City and CORE became embroiled in a heated legal battle. I realized that all was lost and the program would be discontinued. So I took the records to court and turned them over to Innis. I was convinced that any organization that was considered militant during the Civil Rights Movement would be eliminated, particularly the Black Panthers or those that had been involved with the Freedom Rides, such as CORE.

Without my advising them what to do, thirty-one of the thirty-five Target City staff members resigned immediately.

Within one year, Target City Youth Program folded.

FAMILY SUPPORT

After leaving Target City, I was out of work. All too soon, I was broke. I had to be certain that my dedicated staff was employed before I was. I ended up working small jobs for more than a year. My family suffered, especially since we had five daughters – Angela, the youngest, was three. I settled for odd jobs here and there and borrowed heavily from my family. My fragile marriage and family stability continued to crumble. However, two of my in-laws, Gerald and Hicky Pugh, unexpectedly came to my house one day to give me some money that was not a loan, but rather a gift. My sisters, brother, and in-laws, remained loyal in spite of all the years it took to repay them.

Since many of Louise and my families were near the same age, there were frequent get-togethers. During the summer, practically every other weekend, I would take Louise and the four children – Linda, Janet, Sheila, and Michele – to visit relatives in Windsor, Virginia, which was about a 225-mile trip. I would pack three cases of beer in a tub covered with ice, since beer was more expensive in Virginia, and leave early Saturday morning. By the time we arrived, Uncle Hyde would have three bushels of crabs steaming in a barrel in the yard, while my aunt and grandmother would be frying crabs and crab cakes, and making crab soup, along with corn on the cob, potato salad, and lima beans or cabbage. We would feast all afternoon, and then I would take an hour nap before our trip home, which began at dark. After buying gas, I would never return home with more than a dime in my pocket. I made sure I at least had enough to make an emergency phone call if necessary, and provided I could find a phone.

At home, Louise and I hosted many parties that lasted most of the night. Dance parties began with the playing of the "Limbo Rock." Everyone lined up while two people held the broom at either end, parallel to the floor. Then, we took turns bending under the broom, body facing up, without touching it or the floor. After each round, the broom would be lowered. If my brother-in-law, Roosevelt Tyler, whom we endearingly called Zack, was there, no one could beat him.

We also played pinochle or poker, and since we were young adults with limited funds, bidding started at a penny and never got higher than a nickel. We played just as hard, as if we were playing for thousands of dollars.

Sometimes we went fishing, played horseshoes, and badminton. Zack would always beat me at horseshoes, but we were even at badminton.

The good times we'd had with our families in the past helped sustain us during this most difficult time, and today, they remain my closest friends.

NEW CAREER

When I was enrolled in the Army Specialized Training Program at Hampton in 1944, I met a gentleman named Walter Dickerson. He, at times, would be in charge of and supervise our class during compulsory study. After the program was discontinued, most of his class was assigned to the 92nd Infantry Division of Arizona and then sent to Italy. Since six of us in my class of thirteen had come directly from civilian life, we had to be assigned to another base for basic training.

Nineteen years later, Walter was working in the Post Office in New Orleans, while I was at the Baltimore City branch. We both also belonged to the same National Alliance of Postal Employees.

Hurricane Betsy, a severe storm, pummeled New Orleans in 1965, resulting in a terrible loss of property and possessions. To Walter's appeal for aid, the Baltimore branch of the Alliance gathered a supply of clothing, food, and furniture, and sent it to them. It was conceded that our branch had sent more than any other in the country.

I saw Walter again later that summer at an Alliance National Convention in Los Angeles, California. Dr. King spoke at one of our luncheons, and we presented him with a donation for his ministry, the Southern Christian Leadership Conference. My delegation was considered the most organized group there.

Walter expressed gratitude for the assistance they had received during the storm. As we discussed our military experience and lives following discharge from the army, we realized we both had five daughters and no sons.

In 1971, when I was in one of my lowest financial and personal positions, Walter called to tell me that the EEOC had established a district office in Baltimore, and asked me if I wanted a job. I didn't hesitate to accept. I would have to take a written test to determine my placement. I was hired as a GS-11, which was the highest grade one could reach without competition.

One year later, I was promoted to GS-12, then the following year, GS-13 as a supervisor. One of the things I learned about my work with the EEOC was that although businesses in the country were declining, the investigations I oversaw demonstrated that a real conspiracy existed between labor unions and the industry. The collusion was designed to keep blacks, especially black men, from the employment opportunities they deserved. A couple of my major investigations involved large companies and the union.

One, in particular, employed a huge percentage of blacks who only worked in certain areas. I had investigated this place before and knew this. A majority of the men in my community worked there. There were a total of about 18,000 employees when I investigated the company, which had been subjected to a previous investigation by another agency. One of the leaders of the investigation, however, was given a position by the company, and the investigation ceased. Surprisingly, it was he who was assigned to escort me when I began my own probe.

When I received the EEO-1 forms and the trend analysis of forms for three to five years prior, I realized the reduction in force had been gradual. For me, it meant that in due time, the plan of the industry was to become more modern, out-sourcing other materials and therefore, decreasing in size. When I decided to take a tour of the facilities, my intention was to peruse the real places where my people worked and the conditions under which they performed. I was offered a bus ride through the territory, along with the company's attorneys and representatives. I wanted to walk, even though it was about a two-mile radius, but they insisted I ride the bus. I was curious to see the incinerator plant, which I understood to have quite hazardous working conditions. When we reached about half a mile from the place, we had to stop at a railroad track. I hopped out of the bus and started walking. Disturbed, they got off the bus, as well, and walked with me.

Coal entered the incinerator plant from ships. It was then beaten on moving belts to reduce it to soot or cinders, before being transported and burned in ovens to produce steel. All the workers I saw in this plant were black, inhaling coal. Unfortunately, this was their daily job, with little chance for advancement.

I went to another place where there were gas tenders on top of box cars. Gas tenders were used to let the gas out from burning oil. I put on a gas mask and hopped up on the train. Even though the workers wore gas masks, they were inhaling this burning gas that had escaped out of its core. One of my friends who worked there, and had told me about the job, had difficulty breathing, and eventually went blind. They sent him to the hospital, where he soon died. Many jobs there were like that.

My investigation was initiated after approximately eighteen employees came to my office to complain about discrimination in the workplace. First, I had to learn a lot about this company and what type of discrimination they were being accused of. I met with the employees in church, and afterwards in their homes or a restaurant. I was dedicated to this job, because I had heard about this company, and how before the Civil Rights laws, blacks worked in one place while whites worked in another. Once the Civil Rights laws became effective, everyone had to take a written or other kind of test for a promotion to a particular position.

Word got out that a federal investigator was there at that massive industrial company, investigating discrimination.

One day, I was reviewing records, when I was informed that an employee had sent word that he wanted this federal investigator to come see him at his job, because he had failed, for the third time, an electrician's test to be classified as an "A." Workers in that department began as a "C," then performed work or passed a test to become a "B." There were no blacks with the "A" classification. I got in the car with the company's representative. Once we arrived and entered the facility, we could hear someone yelling, "He's over there ranting and raving. He wants to see this investigator!"

This particular open building looked to be about 20,000 square feet. As I walked through it, he moved into a corner pacing up and down. All these whites were looking around while working, and kind of smirking. I walked over to where they were.

"He's down there because he couldn't pass the test," they said, pointing in his direction.

"What kind of test?" I asked.

"All he had to do was wire this diesel engine until it starts. Then he would pass."

"Where are the records of those who passed?" I wanted to know.

They admitted having records.

"How are they being kept?" I asked.

"In this file cabinet, in alphabetical order."

"You have records of everybody?" I asked again.

"Yeah."

"So you want him to put together this diesel engine so it'll work?"

"Mm-mm-mm."

I knew it was difficult to set wires correctly from the battery to the resistor to the coil to the alternator to the starter and the plugs.

"You've got records of everybody?" I repeated.

"Yeah."

"And is this test to be classified as an 'A'?"

"Yeah."

"May I see the records?"

They gave them to me. "Are there any other tests to be taken to become an 'A'?"

"Yeah, there are other tests."

"So how else can you become classified as an 'A'?"

The answer was that if the supervisor decides you can become classified, then you're promoted. I looked at every other record first. I noticed that no one else had to take this particular test the black employee had failed. They were either classified by the

283

supervisor, who granted them competency, or they took another easier test. I perused additional records and discovered that no white employee had been required to take that particular test either.

When I realized I had caught them, and that the union had backed their discriminatory behavior, they called me a "damn Colombo."

I returned on another day, when there was a test for another operation whereby it was an exact simulation of the work. There were certain molds operated by pushing specific buttons. The union agreed that even though no blacks had worked there, anyone who did, had to pass a certain test. The applicant was to enter the room where there was a small-scale replication of what was out on the work floor. Each person was given seven hours of on-the-job instruction. All the whites had passed the test, but no black person could pass. I wondered how blacks could work up there for seven hours and fail, while all the whites passed. Finally, after talking with them, they admitted they were taught off the clock and informally at home. So, I wrote that up. There was so much conspiracy around there that blacks didn't have a chance.

Another issue I discovered was that when there was a reduction in the workforce, there was a reverse seniority consideration. In other words, workers would elevate from Class "C" to "B" to "A," based on seniority. I met with people who drew a diagram for me. I understood at that point that when there was a layoff, it was done by overall seniority in the grade rather than seniority in the company. It meant that if someone had just become a Class "A," and the company had a reduction in force, since that person had just gotten there, he would be the first to leave, even though he may have overall company seniority. The union had agreed to that practice.

As a result of my investigation, the company awarded some of the black employees a small settlement. Many complained that the funds were not enough, while others refused to cash their checks in protest.

The company later closed down.

THE CALL TO MINISTRY

My first memory of church goes back to when I was around five years old. It was during the Christmas season, and we had a Christmas program at our Baptist church that required all the little kids to give a recitation. I was sitting on a bench with a few other boys in my first grade class. Finally, a dark brown Santa Claus came in all dressed in red and white. The boy sitting next to me, out of nowhere, said Santa cleaned the outhouses. I wondered what he did when the toilet holes filled up, but I kept it to myself. At that time, the church was actually a little house on Avondale Road, a street without sewage. So, the bathrooms were actually outhouses.

The next thing I remember, I was around six years old when the church moved from the house on Avondale Road to a one-story building with a different pastor. The men of the congregation had gotten together and decided to build the church, which excited everyone. I felt this was a major accomplishment because during the Great Depression, men were only working at their jobs one or two days a week. They poured cement, laid cinder blocks, did the carpentry work, and installed the windows and electricity. Since the street where this new church was being built had sewage, the men did the plumbing and installed two bathrooms. One member was such a good carpenter that he built a first class podium.

I remember my mother and other women making homemade ice cream and cakes, cooking dinners, and selling them to the community to raise money for the new church. It was a lot of fun because we kids had an excuse to visit each other.

Most of us had begun attending Sunday school at a very young age. That was one turning point for me. My group had such a good teacher, Mrs. Margaret Abbott. She was always prompt, prepared and pleasant. She taught with excitement and dignity. She appeared to us as a real Christian role model. She was one of the main reasons I had wanted to be baptized. The men attended Sunday school and had a class of their own in the rows in the left corner of the little church. They were so dedicated, that we boys talked about how involved they were, and we admired them for it.

One man really stood out. Coleman Henry was friendly and had a sincere appreciation for little things. He was also a dedicated family man. Anytime there was a fundraiser for something, such as a piano, chairs, table, benches, etc., he would walk the entire community to collect any little contribution. Sometimes, we only had a penny or nickel, and he would smile and laugh as if he had received a whole dollar. He never owned a car, always walked and smiled, and lived to be about ninety-four years old. I wanted to be a Christian and a role model to the youth as he was.

In 1936, when I was ten years old, I was baptized by the new pastor, who had been there almost six months. In those days, it was the policy that when a child reached ten, he or she could make an independent decision about baptism.

Two years later, one of the deacon's daughters died from blood poisoning after slipping on a rusty nail. One of her sisters, who was sixteen, became pregnant by the pastor when he visited the grieving family. She left our little community to stay with Aunt Gladys and Uncle Leslie, my mother's sister and brother, until she had the baby. I never heard what happened to her after that. The pastor was terminated, and a new one was appointed, eventually becoming equally bold with his extra-curricular activities.

After the third pastor settled in, I joined the young people's choir for the sole purpose of socializing. As young teenagers, we formed a group to sponsor some events. First, we put on a play in church. Then we organized a singing group. World War II began in 1941, when I was fifteen. Our group decided we would have some kind of debate in the church. I suggested a topic: "Should the black man fight beside the white man in the war?"

We all chose positions, studied and had private reviews with our organizer. We were told we could have our debate in the church as part of an afternoon program. We arrived at the beginning of the program and sat patiently in the back on the last row waiting for the call to participate.

Finally, our leader asked an usher to find out when we could expect to be called. She went up front and whispered to the pastor, and came back with this message. "We can't talk about that because the police might arrest us."

I was extremely angry, and said to myself, *We've got an Uncle Tom on our hands.*

I could not disrespect an elder, but I knew that the police station was more than a mile away and rarely came to the community because there was no crime. The pastor was dismissed a few years later, and still another pastor was elected. I later realized he also had some issues.

All my life I had been going to church to socialize. For many reasons, I was disappointed with the ministers and zealous Christians. Except for about three occasions, all of my major conflicts with people of my race had involved ministers and Christians. I was very much aware of some flaws that had historically haunted church leadership.

My most enjoyable experience at my church centered on my friends, whom I had known most of my life. I had grown up at this Shiloh Baptist Church, and long after I had moved away from Turners, Louise and I still remained members and sang in the choir with our childhood friends. We never learned much biblically, but it was a great place for us to bring our children and socialize.

In 1977, while I was working at the EEOC, some parishioners began intimating that I should become a deacon because the church was falling apart. They were aware of my involvement in civil rights, the labor union, Target City, and the federal government. So they were more encouraged by my potential professional contribution as opposed to any spiritual affect that I could have made.

In the fall of that year, my pastor called me to say he wanted to talk to me. That Sunday, he and his wife came over. Our wives chatted, while he and I went into the basement, and talked for the next eight hours. He admitted that the church was in a state of decline because of him. He had been battling alcohol addiction and felt I had a good reputation.

The only answer I could give, even after all those hours of friendly discussion, was, "I'll think about it."

Three days later, I was driving Louise and her friend, Bertha, to choir rehearsal. Louise was sitting in the front passenger seat, while Bertha was in the back seat, directly behind her. We were driving along Highway 695, which only had two lanes. Today, it has three and four lanes going in both directions. I was driving around 60 mph on the highway with no passing lane. As I drove around a curve in the direction of a long bridge about a mile away, I noticed two huge trucks racing side by side, barreling toward me. One truck was in my lane. I only had a few seconds to think.

I wanted to stop, but I was afraid at that speed my car may slide sideways. If I veered off the road on the gravel, I thought I might lose control, hit the steel fence on the side of the road, and bounce back onto the highway, totally out of control.

About three seconds before we could collide, the truck in my lane began moving toward the fence. I immediately pointed my car to the center of the highway and raced between the two trucks. The truck in my lane went halfway off the road, and the truck on my left moved a little to the right. I hit the gas pedal a little harder and shot right between them. My wife and her friend were talking so intently that they did not realize what had happened.

As I looked in the mirror, the trucks had screeched to a halt, but I had kept on going. I dropped Louise and Bertha off at the church and drove to my sister's house, about three blocks away. When I arrived, my feet were trembling uncontrollably. I just sat quietly, reminiscing about what had just taken place, never saying a word to my sister about it. Once I got myself together, I knew God had spoken to me, and I whispered back, "I got the message."

I called the pastor early the next morning to say that I would become a deacon. When it was revealed in the church that I was a candidate, Louise's young cousin, Rose Marie, and her husband, Jonathan, drove up to our house from Turners one day offering to have Bible study with me every Friday evening for nine months, the same amount of time required for me to train for ordination. I readily accepted. Louise informed me that she would not support my becoming a deacon. Although Rose Marie was a first cousin, when they came to our house every Friday, she would go into the bedroom and close the door until they left about an hour later.

When I was finally ordained in June 1978, the trustees called me into their office to say they were glad to see me, because they wanted me to help them get rid of the pastor. I knew his problems. I asked if he was fired, would he be eligible for Social Security. The answer was no, because they had never reported his earnings. I also wanted to know if he had medical insurance. Again, the answer was no. When he was sick, they would take up an offering. His main illness was alcoholism, and they had not sought help for him.

I told the trustees I would not assist in firing anyone unless I had done what I could to at least try to reverse the circumstances. I took my pastor to my accountant to file taxes so he would be eligible for Social Security in seven years. The accountant enrolled him in a group insurance program. I helped him get admitted into a rehabilitation center. I had successfully completed my first assignment as a deacon.

RETIREMENT

My job description rose to a new level when the EEOC requested I lead a team in two states; the one in my home city of Baltimore, and another in Pittsburg, Pennsylvania. I took the first morning flight out of Baltimore every Monday to go to a certain company. I would check into a hotel and arrive at the office around three hours later. I would then meet with the team, teach investigative techniques, and exchange ideas with them on improving their performance. While an investigation was going on, I would work with them in their homes, or go out and train them until Tuesday night. Then I'd take a Wednesday flight back to Baltimore and return to the office there. I would meet with my team on Friday to review their work, socialize, and plan for the following week. I would work alone on Saturday to complete a subjective review of the work for submission to the director for approval, signature, and mailing. I continued this routine for about six months. Through that type of work, I witnessed the growth and demise of companies, in terms of employment.

I realized that every company I investigated could not tolerate a strong black male. When I found one in any good position, he would be the one person filing charges of harassment and humiliation, the failure to be given adequate responsibilities, or the employer resisting his personality and authority. What the whites wanted, and what a black man was required to be in order to be accepted, was an "Uncle Tom." I did not experience any encouragement for a strong-willed black male. The companies may have tolerated a strong black female, but in all my years of investigations, I had never witnessed any type of support for their male counterpart. Even if they acted as though they were competent in their work capabilities, their authority was almost always neutralized.

When a training school was formed in Philadelphia, five of us were chosen to train all investigators in the country. We were: Al Harris from Philadelphia, Kathy Stokes from Newark, and George Dredden, Vivian Dixon, and me, from Baltimore. We enjoyed meeting other investigators around the country. Trainees would come in for about four days, and we would teach them what we knew. For me, it was a wonderful learning experience.

After being promoted to compliance manager in Baltimore, a director's position became available in the Newark office, and I bid on it. I did not realize it at the time, but was later informed, that the office was scheduled for closing because of the conflict between blacks, whites, and Hispanics. When I arrived, I got the staff together, taught them how to investigate and monitor their own performance, which made it a more productive office. I received two awards for good leadership. During the Reagan Administration, there were forty-seven district offices around the country. There were three offices that had an increase in staff. My office was one of them. We progressed from fourteen to a twenty-one-member staff in the four years I was there.

Finally, one day my personal convictions hit me like a boulder. There would never be enough resources for civil rights agencies to provide equal healthcare for all, nor equal educational and employment opportunities. The government would not put enough financial capital into equal employment opportunities to have an impact. We were processing a lot of cases, probably too many for the available resources; cases that needed their day in court to reach a resolution. People were suffering economically, and jobs were not available. There were no remedies. The courts were so crowded, they couldn't handle their cases quickly enough to be effective.

I realized that the majority of agencies that stood up for civil rights were not allocated sufficient resources to service countless complaints. Many offices were situated in areas that made it difficult for the people they could serve to access their facilities. The offices only operated during the day, the same time major businesses operated. The majority of people lived in outlying areas. There were only one or two offices in every state. What were these people in the outlying areas going to do? If they were going to file charges of discrimination, how did they become aware of their rights in the first place? In my mind, justice delayed is justice denied.

One Friday morning, I decided to retire without notice, and not go back to that office another day. That was it. I was gone.

DIVORCE AND REMARRIAGE

Louise decided she would not support my involvement in the ministry. Our marriage had deteriorated and spiraled into a vicious cycle that caused irreparable damage. So, within a couple of years of becoming a deacon, I was also in the process of becoming divorced.

I anonymously began a serious search for a future wife. First, I set up my criteria. I wanted a woman who had a college education, a job and a loving family of at least two children, and was also divorced. I didn't want a Christian, though, because I considered them to be too self-righteous, hypocritical, and not community oriented. During my frequent travels around the country, I would discreetly ask questions to determine if there was someone in whom I'd be interested, based on my criteria. I was unsuccessful for quite some time.

About three years later, I found someone right under my nose. Jackie had all the qualities I was looking for, except that she happened to be a Christian and belonged to the same church.

One Sunday, while sitting in the choir facing the congregation, I saw a young lady I had known almost all her life walk into the church with her two young children, a 4-year-old son and 8-year-old daughter. I had worked with her on the church's fiftieth anniversary celebration, and I had taught a few classes that she attended. However, I never thought of her in any way except as an associate.

I knew she and her husband were separated. As usual, she came in smiling, and I began to notice even more how well she related to her family, whom I knew well. When her father relocated from Virginia to get a job in the 1930s, he stayed in our house for about seven years. In fact, he bought me my first suit with long pants.

After this particular service, I went up to her and said, "You belong to me. You are mine. My mind is made up."

She eyed me and delivered a smile that said, *"You must be joking."*

I had wanted someone with children because I was near the age of being able to retire with minimal federal and social security benefits. I didn't want to leave this life without some African American children or spouse being able to receive the eligible funds as dependents and survivors.

During my divorce proceedings, I had been fortunate enough to be appointed as director of the EEOC office in Newark, New Jersey, and immediately relocated. A year later, I joined the Calvary Baptist Church in Red Bank in 1984, and was immediately installed as a deacon. Pastor John C. Smith was my greatest supporter and friend.

Before I left Baltimore, I confided in four people about my intention to marry Jackie; her Uncle Howard Allmond, two of my best friends with whom we had risked our careers for each other at one time or another, Haywood and Myrtle Bryant, and Jackie's mother. I met with them separately three nights in a row.

We were so broke because of legal fees spent on both of our divorces, child support, and other obligations, that we could not pay for a wedding. The members of Calvary Baptist gifted us with this event. I wore one of my old white suits, and Jackie wore a Sunday dress. Her uncle gave her away and bought us a case of champagne. Sadly, he died two months later, which caught us off guard because I didn't know he had been ill.

We became very active in the ministry. The church bought a bus and we took the youth group on several trips, including Disney World in Florida. The next year we took them to Canada and Niagara Falls, then Luray Caverns of Virginia, Colonial Williamsburg, Busch Gardens Amusement Park, and King's Dominion. Rev. Smith drove the bus on each trip.

I began conducting Bible classes, teaching Sunday school, and conducting prayer service. Additionally, I was delivering at least thirty baskets of food each month to the needy.

In the late 1980's, Jackie and I began keeping our grandchildren and their cousins from age three to thirteen for two weeks every summer. The first year, twenty-seven children stayed with us. Along with Vacation Bible School, we would take them swimming, horseback riding, and to other childhood activities. We eventually built an entire playground and in-ground pool in our backyard for them to use when they came to visit.

During that first summer, some of the children got sick with colds and other ailments. Their diets had consisted of punch, ice cream, and other junk foods because that's what they enjoyed. One by one, the children started feeling bad, and Jackie would hold them from time to time to the point where I could see that she was about to get sick also. We decided to change their diets. First, I lined them up and gave them each a teaspoon of cod liver oil. Breakfast was most important. We served them oatmeal or other warm cereal, eggs, and vitamin C drinks. They ate fresh fruit, tuna or salmon for lunch. We also shied away from fried foods. All meals were served on schedule, three times a day, and all the children got well.

We have kept children for at least a week every summer since then, and we have never had another illness with them. We concluded that based on their behavior and overall health status, many of the children in schools do not receive a healthy diet on a consistent basis.

The people and Pastor Smith began saying I was called to be a preacher. I was extremely afraid but knew I wasn't going through two damn trucks again. I felt so inferior for that position that I sought out our best and nearest seminary on recommendation by Pastor Smith.

YOU CAN RUN, BUT YOU CAN'T HIDE

As scared as I was then and now of what I perceive as abiding by the will of God, I still didn't feel qualified to be either a preacher or a pastor. I knew that preaching meant interpreting the Scriptures, and I did not know enough about them to do that.

My daughter, Janet, and her husband, Euvon, were living in California during the 1980s. They had become members of an integrated non-denominational church that they claimed was very organized and had a young, outreach pastor, through whom many people were experiencing a change in their lives. The church, therefore, attracted many new members, especially the youth. I had also witnessed positive changes in Janet and Euvon's lifestyle. When they shared with me the impact their church had on them, I immediately traveled to their home and stayed with them for several weeks. I frequented their church not only to worship, but to study how that church was run.

One of the most important things their pastor did was give expository Bible teaching and study in an informal manner. The dress code was more relaxed, as opposed to the dressy attire required by many denominational churches. I invested all my money in their collection of books to prepare myself, even before entering the seminary.

Still, I felt inadequate and needed more knowledge to be more effective in ministry. I knew, too, that I had to study counseling. In reality, though, I had no desire to be a preacher or pastor and felt so unprepared, I wanted to duck. However, I was reminded of what happened to heavyweight boxing champion, Joe Louis. Before WWII, he fought Billy Conn of Pittsburgh, who was lighter than he, but fast on his feet. He had also won all the rounds running around the ring until he made a mistake, and Joe Louis, luckily, knocked him out in the thirteenth round and maintained his title of the world's heavyweight champion.

A few years later, a rematch was scheduled. People began kidding Louis by telling him that Billy would run him to death and win the rematch. Joe responded with these appropriate words that relate to my reluctance to becoming a minister: "He can run, but he can't hide." Remembering that incident, I concluded that I wanted to run the wrong way.

I decided to attend New Brunswick Theological Seminary. I wanted the best education possible to prepare me for this journey. Just before I entered the seminary, my youngest granddaughter died at the age of six weeks.

When I started school, I took two of the most difficult courses I'd ever had, Greek and Old Testament History. As my mid-term exams approached, my oldest grandson died after a lengthy battle with leukemia, and I was devastated. He was just sixteen years old. My instructors told me I could postpone the exams until after his funeral. But since I knew the subjects and assumed I was well-prepared, I took them anyway. I received the lowest scores I had ever achieved in my life. My grade in Greek was in the 50s, and in the Old Testament, in the 60s. That ruined my GPA, and for the first time, I graduated with a 3.19.

I knew the answers, but my mind could not process them. I realized that many of our black youth see violence at home, and fights and deaths of relatives and friends, then must go to school and try to learn. The public school administration does not realize the trauma the students experience in their neighborhoods and homes because of domestic violence, home arrests, and poverty. Having been a member of the school leadership council and attended many school-based and staff meetings, I realized there are not enough professionals in the public schools to adequately serve the many children who live every day in a catastrophic atmosphere.

SUMMER OF 1987

After the end of the second semester, the seminary sponsored a trip to Holland for students who wanted to attend a two-week session on "Suffering and Salvation." The sessions were held at the University of Leiden with presenters from different faiths. There is a common thread that weaves through most religions that says, "As you wish men do unto you, do ye also unto them."

The presenters also discussed their beliefs regarding death and salvation. I was pleased during those two weeks that Jackie had accompanied me on the trip. We made certain that we attended every session, and every excursion. We visited the Red Light District in Amsterdam where women can freely advertise their skills. However, they had to pass a physical examination every year, and keep their houses very clean. We must remember that during WW II, Holland was quickly overrun by the Germans, and the last country freed from the Germans. Most of the male population had been either killed in battle or taken prisoner by the Germans, and died in captivity. Pro stations were built in every major city in the U.S. to prevent servicemen from getting diseases, while United Service Organizations were designated so that females could entertain them.

We also visited a large church in Amsterdam that allowed the homeless to stay there during the night, but they had to leave at dawn. There were designated staff members to monitor the facilities at night.

After returning from Holland, Jackie and I drove to California to visit my daughter, Janet, and son-in-law, Euvon, and attend their church. Since I had to commute to school, I had bought a 1986 Nissan pickup truck and put a cover over the back so the children could ride there. As much as I tried to teach her, Jackie could not learn how to drive a stick shift. We agreed that I would drive six to eight hours. Then I would point the truck toward the highway so she could get in and put one foot on the clutch and the other on the accelerator and release the brake, push the clutch in, and I would shift the gears. She would then drive four or five hours while I slept. We left early Saturday morning and arrived in Los Angeles on Monday night.

We took our children and grandchildren to Mexico, where we had so much fun shopping. We also visited the Grand Canyon.

EXPLORING DENOMINATIONS

During my second year in the seminary, I volunteered to gain experience in another church – a Reformed church in Jersey City, where I served for five months. After attending some meetings and a quarterly conference, I realized the Reformed denomination had one of the better management systems.

During the next semester, I volunteered to serve at another Baptist church. At the end of the semester, the members gave me and my wife a mirror with a Japanese estate engraving, for which there was a patent, and therefore, the design could not be duplicated.

While studying theology, I was convinced that salvation is a gift from God, rather than the rituals instituted by various religions. I knew I could not preach that a person must be submerged in water in order to be saved, as was taught in my Baptist church in Turners Station. I then sought to join another denomination.

Fortunately, I was taking some courses with Rev. Archie Richmond, pastor of an African Methodist Episcopal Church in Atlantic Highlands, New Jersey. Not only did we take some classes together, but we would frequently meet at the library and study together for six to eight hours. He encouraged me to join his church and denomination, because we had a mutual respect for each other, and we were both secure in our pastoral roles.

Incidentally, Jackie always accompanied me wherever I went without hesitation or complaint. She also sacrificed and paid the tuition for all the degrees I received without one question. She is an exceptional Christian. Wherever I was assigned, the members seemed to love her more than they did me. I am extremely fortunate to have someone who accepted my decisions about where to worship without question or resistance.

CLINICAL PASTORAL EDUCATION

I took Clinical Pastoral Education during my last year at New Brunswick Theological Seminary, which I truly enjoyed because it included working in hospitals. We were challenged to serve as many people as possible, and keep a journal of our prayers and discussions. We would then review them with our supervisors on a weekly basis.

Once I was eating lunch in the cafeteria, and a woman was sobbing to herself. I approached her quietly and introduced myself. After a few minutes, a code blue was announced. It was her husband, who had passed away that quickly. The doctors brought us into her husband's room so she could spend some time with him before they transported him to the morgue. After a few moments, I invited her to the chapel. She explained that her husband had been bisexual, but he was better than anyone she had ever known. I just accepted the fact that happiness is better than bitter judgment.

Near the end of one semester, we had to assemble as a group with a supervisor. I was the only black in the group of eight. We were all eager to be church pastors. We were asked what turning point in our lives had motivated us toward the ministry. Each person before me shared an incident that had influenced them to become a minister; such as parents separating, the inability to become pregnant, losing a parent, etc. I shared that I had buried my father and mother, lost my oldest brother to TB, and had recently lost my youngest granddaughter and oldest grandson.

All except two in the group criticized me and accused me of trying to manipulate them because "nobody can take that much." I was furious, but never said a word. I came to understand that some people are blessed enough not to experience many tragedies in their lifetime. It seems almost impossible for those who haven't to be able to empathize with those who have.

I believed that if a pastor cannot empathize that way, then the members of his or her congregation will adopt the same attitude. The time I spent serving on the Baltimore Grand Jury, driving a cab, working in the labor union, and counseling those involved in domestic violence, convinced me that many leaders who have not suffered cannot believe the hardships and pressures that many of the people they serve must cope with, while trying to go to school, work, or rely on public assistance to survive.

THEOLOGY OF PASTORAL COUNSELING

After obtaining the Master of Divinity degree with a 3.18 average, I realized I still didn't know enough to be the pastor I had envisioned. I believed it was one thing to be a preacher, to exhort, to interpret Scripture, and to acquire effective delivery of a message; but it's another to be a pastor, to save even one sheep. I'm not minimizing the importance and blessedness of good preaching, but it alone is insufficient. Our race has been afflicted with an increase in intra-racial crime. Along with an increase in churches, there is a simultaneous increase in the prison population. There is also a decreasing percentage of black-owned businesses. I've noticed that if there is a business owned by blacks, patronizing and support are minimal. It has also been reported that the ratio of the black male population in colleges and universities has decreased from one male to four females around fifteen years ago, to one male to eight females now. We need some drastic changes in all of our institutions.

Having worked in an agency to uphold the law, it is obvious to me as to the direction in which we are now headed. Our people need personal and confidential guidance on how to grow mentally, physically, economically, and spiritually. We need to know how our ancestors survived in the midst of slavery and oppression. We also need to remember that just as Darfur in Africa has been a battleground of blacks against blacks, it is a throwback to what happened years ago when Africans sold fellow Africans to white slave traders, trying to profit from the sacrifice of a neighbor.

I felt that knowing the Bible and being able to preach are not enough. During my investigation of discrimination in employment, every preacher I met refused to even give a confidential statement to help a member of his or her congregation resolve an issue that the preacher knew about. I'd rather see a sermon any day than hear one.

I enrolled in the New Brunswick Seminary's Master's Program in the Theology of Pastoral Care and Counseling Program, the most informative course I've ever studied. It addressed private and group counseling for addiction. We had to report on the counseling we had completed each week and critically assess each other's performance.

One of the things we learned is that if you've regularly been around a friend or family member with an addiction, you should enroll in Al-Anon and complete the steps. It is not recommended to develop a relationship with someone of the opposite sex in the same program. Jackie and I have both experienced familial addiction, compelling us to form a group in the church. We continued the program for four years. More whites attended than blacks.

MY FIRST CHURCH

Meanwhile, I was assigned to a little church in a community that reminded me of my small town of Turners Station. Naturally, I enjoyed myself there. I visited everyone's home. We rotated Bible classes and meetings in people's homes. Jackie and I took some of the children to the park and to the Congress of Christian Education at Delaware State College. We marked off a wooded area on the church property, excavated it, and got approval for the space to become a parking lot and playground.

We became so close as a church family that one of the member's relatives in Southern New Jersey drove up to the church with his bus and band to participate in the annual picnic. The entire community came out and had a good time. I had been warned that the relative was living with two women, one black and one white. Supposedly, they were very happy. A few years later, I preached at this church and was informed that he and one of the women had died. The survivor was supposedly doing well in spite of it.

Eventually, I was assigned to another church. When I arrived, I found the door to every office was locked, as if there were a million dollars in each room, including the pastor's office, the communion room, the finance room, and the choir room. I told them that I operate on trust; so they would have to remove the locks and turn in the keys. They were assured that they would be kept abreast of our financial records, and unless I was in a meeting, I would be available to each member. For two years, I had my meetings and conducted Bible classes, but no member would volunteer to come to my office, which was always open.

I had previously joined the Ministerial Alliance, which had been organized for years. The Honorable Mark Apostolou came to one of our meetings requesting our assistance. He said he was hearing and processing an inordinate amount of domestic violence cases. He wanted the ministers to volunteer to counsel some of the families involved, thereby allowing him to reduce the number of enormous fines and incarcerations, while attempting to resolve some of the key issues that precipitated the problem in the first place.

I was a rather new person in the group; so, I wanted to see if someone else would respond, and I would have been happy to support them. When no one did, I approached the judge and offered to try. We entered into an agreement and developed procedures we thought would be effective.

Initially, I would counsel up to three or four cases a night. The people would come to my church office, because while attending seminary, I came to believe that counseling by a minister may be more effective in a house of worship rather than in an office building. They would invariably ask me in a hostile manner, "What do you want with me?"

I immediately developed a form to use to break the ice, and then I would draw a genogram of three generations. After about a year, people would come in my office, talking freely. Invariably, some started confiding that one or more of their relatives were members of my church. Since these cases were confidential, I never acted differently toward my church members and told them not one word about my extra duties. Gradually, they began coming to my office to discuss one thing or another, I believe, to see how I would respond and handle their issues, as well as if I would betray their confidence.

In about a year, members began flocking to my office on any given day to discuss their problems. I really enjoyed it because it gave me more insight into the daily pressures of my people and how they tried to cope, with few resources. An old Native American proverb states, "Never criticize a man until you have walked a mile in his moccasins."

I have counseled more than one thousand cases for domestic violence, which have included black and white, gay and lesbian, and interracial couples. I have found that the issues are basically the same – infidelity, control, finances, education, and family. The sad thing I would hear was that often when the police, both black and white, would come to their home to make an arrest, they would throw the father or adult male to the floor, put a foot on his back, and handcuff him in front of the children. Then the children would have to attend school the following day and be expected to be a model student.

Most of the time, attendance officers in the schools did not know how to earn the confidence of the students so that they could really share their private concerns. Many had relatives and friends arrested and/or killed; however, in the community where the church is located, I never heard of a large number of counselors being available for students as there are in suburban schools.

As a matter of fact, one day shots were fired near a school about two hours before the end of the school day. What did the administrators do? With the consent of the local school board, they closed the schools early and allowed the students to be in harm's way rather than have a school lockdown and invite counselors in to help them cope with their fears.

COMMUNITY SERVICE

In another one of my pastoral assignments, I met a Muslim who expressed respect for my tolerance. Some of his children had participated in a Kwanza celebration in our church. He came to me stating that he had to move from his rental home because the owner of the home claimed to need the property for himself.

The Muslim said he moved into a larger house a half block from the church, in a neighborhood that was surrounded by drug dealers. There were also gaps in the house through which he could see the outside. He said that since he could not save enough for a down payment, there was a house with nineteen rooms in a good neighborhood that he wanted me to buy for his family and him, and he would rent with the option to buy it.

I knew he had a secure job with the municipality, so I agreed to purchase the house so he and his family could move in. After settlement, all his rent checks were rejected, and I had to make the mortgage payments for four years. Finally, I told him I needed some work done to the property, and couldn't make any more payments. Someone wanted to buy it, and I agreed to sell it. He finally moved, and I sold the house. Even though I paid his rent for years, he has not spoken to me since. He also failed to clean the property for the sale, which he had agreed to do. So, I had to hire people to make the house livable by the day of settlement.

I don't believe there is any religion in which all members are honorable. But, the Lord blessed my wife and me. After I sold the house, I was able to have an enclosed porch and deck built onto my home and pay cash for a new automobile. I have always believed that if I try to help others, the Lord will bless me.

RELIGIOUS PASSIVITY

One of the greatest disasters I've witnessed from a so-called church occurred in the community where I was pastor. The school district was and still is losing its effectiveness to encourage education, thereby stimulating the increase in crime. Of the approximately twenty-five churches in Asbury Park, New Jersey, only three of us ministers were regular attendees at the school board meetings. We also served on the school leadership committees to encourage the students and support the policies that were beneficial to improving their performance.

Many of the members of the Board of Education did not have any children in the schools. As ministers, the three of us were trying to support the parents who really were interested in their children's performance. What did the leaders of one AME church do? They warned the pastor that they were not paying him to get involved in education and requested he be replaced. He was relocated to a community that wanted a pastor who would be interested in their community. The question is, have the members forgotten why the AME church was formed? It was formed out of a protest to discrimination.

To me, it is a disgrace when people are more interested in their titles and positions than in the lives of citizens, particularly the youth they represent. If that is the position of a church, then Satan has really infiltrated its environment.

I wonder what would have happened if the pastor had remained. Maybe some citizens would have appreciated a church with more boldness. Jesus, in Matthew 13:25, said to let those rough tares and good wheat grow together. Once they are fully grown, remove the tares and burn them; then reward yourself with the wheat.

Just to have a large number of egotistical, non-community minded members is counterproductive to the service of our people and God.

If I had the authority, I would have left the pastor where he was and told the congregation to abide by the commitment for community development or find a church that did not care. I would rather have twenty progressive members than ninety "Uncle Toms." Neither the church nor the community will ever be effective catering to haughtiness. Our communities are falling apart because of the rule of pacifying selfishness. I'd rather have ten sharp shooters than ninety soldiers who don't know how to load a rifle.

THE NEGATIVE INFLUENCE OF THE TEACHERS' UNION

One of the most disappointing experiences I have had was what I perceived as the deliberate and systemic destruction of the lives of the African American family in Asbury Park. In 1993, there was an organized influential group of African American citizens called the Asbury United. The organization had developed pride and motivation for the citizens of the town, and the parents, families and children were highly motivated.

Jackie and I, along with our two young children, Marguerite and Roland, began attending the annual convention of the New Jersey Education Association (NJEA), the Teachers' Union, in Atlantic City, New Jersey. This convention was very attractive in promoting the involvement of students in the annual affair.

Generally, there was a panel of teachers and students from Asbury Park, among other schools, to demonstrate and discuss their accomplishments as role models for the other schools. We were so impressed that we attended the high school graduation ceremonies. The graduating class consisted of at least 180 students of the 200 or more that had graduated from the middle school.

Although the population has remained constant, the initial enrollment in the elementary school has been the same until recently. Even though the number of students entering high school is the same, less than 100 are now graduating. There have been many relevant changes. At first, the superintendent in this predominately African American community was Dr. Antonio

Lewis, an African American male. Four of the five principals in the school system were also African American, as were the majority of the School Board members.

The Teachers' Union became more involved in the district and developed a stronger influence on the local school board. The new principals hired were predominantly white; the number of white teachers also increased. Because of the decline in student achievement, a special team designated by the Department of Education investigated the school district. The investigation graded the performance of the school district in five categories, with a score of 50 or less, indicating failure. Dr. Lewis received the highest evaluation of 70, the only one above a score of 50. The Board members, which by this time, consisted of loyal union members and whites, received a rating of less than 20. Still, the Board fired Dr. Lewis. About twenty of us went to the Department of Education to complain and demand his reinstatement, to the Governor's office and the State's Attorney's office, to no avail.

After that, Dr. Lewis finally took his case to court. The court awarded him with a position as principal because he had tenure. The parents became so frustrated with the actions of the Board of Education, they began staying away from the polls.

We organized efforts to change the composition of the School Board. We provided cars to transport voters to and from the voting polls, but it became rare to encourage even 200 people to vote. In other words, the present system had completely discouraged the African Americans in a small town of about 16,000 residents. They had given up to this atmosphere of hopelessness.

A distressing result has been that the number of gangs has grown, and the number of children getting arrested has increased to the extent that they have been relocated to a larger penal system in another county. Parents, therefore, have less contact and opportunity to support their children.

I know all my efforts to help the community of Asbury Park have been unsuccessful against a force with its own agenda. I had once been a dedicated member of the National Alliance of Postal Employees, but I had also dedicated myself to equality for all.

DOCTORATE OF MINISTRY

Having earned my second master's degree, I was convinced I needed to enroll in the Doctor of Ministry program at Drew University. Things went smoothly until it was time to prepare for my thesis. I was required to take a particular course. After a few weeks, I realized the professor was emitting some negative vibes toward me, even though my work was always on time. Several students noticed as well, and asked me why it was so obvious that he didn't care for me. I didn't know, but since the subject was required, I had to adjust.

Simultaneous to the necessity of coping with the professor's hostility, I had asked another pastor to assist me in getting an appointment as pastor of a church so I could make the changes necessary to write my thesis. I was assigned to St. James AME Church, a small church in Englishtown, New Jersey, with about twelve members. Most of them were descendants of ancestors who had been slaves, and were forced to migrate to New Jersey to work on farms owned by whites. Their little area was called Woodville. Along with gardens, livestock and chickens, they eventually had their own businesses – a store, barber shop, night club, shoe repair shop, ball field, and church. The church was built before the Civil War. In keeping with the Southern tradition, the cemetery was placed right next to it, which prevented it from expanding.

On my first Sunday, it was easy to determine from the commotion I heard after the service had ended about the little finances received, that there were two factions in the church. The very next day, I made some temporary changes to control the finances until I could determine the skills, dedication, and professionalism of the church members, which angered the majority of them. Not long after, I began having chest pains and drove myself to the hospital. X-rays revealed that my main aorta was ninety-nine percent closed, and I had to have emergency quadruple bypass. I was discharged after one week and spent two weeks in rehab. After that, I was housebound for more than a month.

In the meantime, one faction of the church called me and demanded we meet in my home while I was rehabilitating. I had to listen for the sake of determining whether their issue was skills or power and recognition. I did not make any changes because I concluded that it was all about recognition and power, rather than service.

While recovering, I also had to withdraw from the professor's class, and enroll in the same class later, with a more relaxed professor, who also happened to be an excellent instructor.

When I returned to church after a two-month absence, I explained that all changes had been made according to the rules in the AME Discipline. Some left. There were no problems after that, and I grew to really enjoy that little church. Its members faithfully supported my effort to earn my degree.

I was transferred to a larger church in August 1993, and received my degree that October. We had a celebration in the new church, Allen Chapel AME Church.

Several years later, I began studying the number of arrests in Asbury Park, and noticed that within a few months, there were more than forty arrests. After a couple of years, I was offered a grant to set up training for other pastors and church leaders to attend to learn the value of counseling. A friend of mine, Rodney

O'Neal, assisted me in writing the proposal, procuring the funds, and assigning the district to monitor the project.

I enlisted my professor from Drew to help me teach one of the classes. All the participants admired his skills and the quality of his ability to plan, organize, and present his material in such a way that didn't appear to be hostile to anyone. I invited all the pastors in the area, which averaged about twenty-two, to attend at no cost. Only three responded and attended the first session. They did not return. I then concentrated on encouraging the parishioners to attend. About eighteen participated in the sessions, which lasted three years. I finally invited Dr. Josephine O'Neal to provide training for the group. She proved to be an excellent instructor. I am constantly reminded of the effects the training at Tuskegee has had on my attitude and behavior that remains: listen to others, care for others, and share with others.

THE DREAM

Considering all the conflicts from the beginning of documented history, analyzing some of the migrations, the rise and fall of empires, and the resulting colors, features, and mixed languages developed for survival, I conclude that God created one race – the human race – and that is what He intended it to be. But the deviation from what God intended is motivated by two extremes – the poverty of those who need assistance to survive, and the hard-nosed greed of those whose motto seems to be "by any means necessary," for them to get to and remain on top.

Caring for each other was one of the major themes emphasized at Tuskegee. If a person in your group was suffering, you must suffer with him. This theme was taught very effectively. If you saw or happened to be in the vicinity of your classmate being disciplined or hazed by any upperclassman, and you did not volunteer to join the plight of your classmate, you would receive more hazing than he did.

In reality, if all the humans on this planet could act as a team, poverty and greed would be eradicated. After WWI, the League of Nations was formed, but we went on to have another war. After WWII, The United Nations was organized, but the effectiveness appears to be limited by the individual agendas of the member-nations.

Jackie and I became members of the Tinton Falls Rotary Club. Among the reasons for my active participation are the efforts of the International Rotary Club to help eliminate polio, globally, and provide assistance in other areas. If Rotarians who, regardless of race, creed, color, or sex can join to eliminate the scourge of polio, why can we not make a joint effort to eliminate poverty and hunger? I just wonder how God will eventually judge us for not being a model for equality rather than greed. It appears that religion is being used to pacify the guilt of selfish transactions, rather than striving to do as Jesus and other prophets did; love and sacrifice for others less fortunate. I believe that if this attitude could be adopted universally, the prison industry would be eliminated or would be the exception rather than the rule.

In some way, love should be encouraged by providing a methodology and benefits that would fuel its flame.

"And Jesus said unto him, 'Thou shalt love the Lord thy God with all thy heart, and with all thy soul, and with all thy mind. This is the first and great commandment. And the second is like unto it, Thou shalt love thy neighbor as thyself. On these two commandments hang all the law and the prophets.'"

Matthew 22:37-40

LESSONS LEARNED FROM THE JEWS

As I study history from the biblical perspective and other writings, I realize the Jews as a people and a faith have suffered as much as, if not more than, other religious and ethnic groups. They have, however, remained a strong force in the world, economically and spiritually. Therefore, I made a commitment to study the manners and customs, as well as the training, discipline, and accomplishments of some of my most important colleagues and friends, the Jews in Baltimore.

I first encountered Jews when I was six years old. My family had moved across the street from a Jewish-owned grocery store. Three blocks from home was the drugstore, also owned by a Jew. What I noticed about both stores was the promptness and efficacy of service. During the Depression era, my mother and I would often go to the store with no money. Miss Sadie, the owner of the grocery store, would let us get a few items. Then she would record the purchase in a little book and allow us to pay later when we were able. She and her family lived in an apartment on the second floor of the store. Their daughter attended school outside of the community because of segregation.

As a young adult, I knew I had to shop at a store owned by Jews to be treated as a human being. I remember when Louise and I got married and bought furniture on credit from a Jewish store. We were allowed to pay for it monthly for nine months before having it delivered. In those days, they didn't charge interest.

I believe it was in the late 1960's that my daughter, Sheila, and I were invited to the then Painters Mills Theater to see a one-man play, based on the story of how the Rothschild family took over the banks in some countries in Europe during the middle of the nineteenth century. The performance was eye-opening. First, the father's original name was Amschel Moses Bauer, and the name was later changed to Rothschild. Amschel set up his five sons in banking houses in different countries.

Sometime in the early 1970s, when I was living in Baltimore County, there was a major case in which a young Jewish girl of around eighteen or nineteen years of age, who worked in a pet shop in a Jewish neighborhood, was brutally murdered. It took several days and intense publicity before the killer was apprehended. It was stated that he was a young Jewish man. I had served on the Baltimore Grand Jury for three months in 1965 and was aware how much publicity was given to trials involving a major crime. I was getting two newspapers every day, seven days a week – the Morning Sun and the Baltimore News American. I couldn't find anything in either paper about the trial and never read another word about the outcome. The only rumor I heard was that no Jewish attorney would represent the accused killer.

When I worked in the Post Office from 1951 to 1966, a Jewish lawyer taught Parliamentary Procedure at my request.

Furthermore, The National Alliance of Postal Employees fought management very hard about discrimination. Management finally issued instructions that no administrator could attend our meetings, even if invited. One Jewish administrator defied the order and attended when invited. He was quiet, but well-informed and dignified.

There was another administrator, the assistant postmaster, who in his own manner, made it known that he did not like blacks. Both of them retired about the same time. We figured it was a conspiracy when both retirement programs were scheduled simultaneously, because normally, administrators were given separate celebrations. When we met next, the strategy of management was discussed at great length. I finally made some motions.

First, the Alliance would purchase a table for ten, realizing that we would be the only blacks present at such a large banquet. That motion quickly passed. Then, I made a motion that the Alliance present a plaque to the Jewish administrator, complimenting him for his fairness and dedication to all employees, and a reprimand to the assistant postmaster for not being polite or caring for people of color.

The Branch was hesitant, but it passed. The president did an excellent job in making the presentation as agreed, as he was just as militant as I. He spoke well and to the point.

When I was director of Target City Youth Program during the Civil Rights era of the 60s, the major theme was Black Power. After the assassination of Dr. King in April, 1968, there were many riots around the country and, of course, in Baltimore. Later, the governor requested a major conference on Crime and Community Responsibility. I was one of the panelists. As I spoke about the responsibility of governments – city, state, and federal – one of the remarks I made with strong emphasis was that the federal government should designate a holiday in honor of Dr. King. A Jewish participant sitting in the front row calmly said, "We don't ask, we take ours." I never again used the term "Black Power," because I realized how few blacks actually participated in the movement. With thousands of black Christian ministers, as well as churches, it appeared to me that there should have been a major change in our direction and methods to further our progress as a people. Some prominent ministers have stated that there is too much praise and worship and not enough liberation.

There were several Jews at different stages in my career at Target City who helped me obtain funds for my projects. A Jewish congressman was instrumental in assisting me in obtaining approval for the printing project, along with the necessary equipment.

Later, we were considering buying a small shopping center in East Baltimore. First, I needed information about how to manage a such a project. At the time, there was a person in Baltimore who had a reputation of owning more property than anyone else. His firm was advertised on many billboards. I made an appointment with him, and he assigned someone to assist me.

After a few days, I was invited to attend a conference by the International Conference of Shopping Centers in Miami Beach. It was well-attended with many displays of quality products. The conference seemed to emphasize the increasing trend toward regional shopping centers. Most of those present were Jews, and I felt special having been invited. Except for my wife, Louise, the great Lionel Hampton band, and me, there were no other blacks in attendance. I marveled at the accomplishments of a people who had also experienced generations of persecution, as well as the Holocaust, under Hitler. I wondered if my people would ever achieve such cohesiveness and power.

The Tuskegee Airmen had the cohesiveness and power necessary to be a strong force in helping other ethnic groups engage in military battle safely and successfully. After the war, we lacked that support, not only from those same ethnicities, but from our own people, to sustain that power, and remain a living example of what can be achieved among a race of people who stand together even in the face of outrage, discrimination, and tragedy. As we sank into obscurity, so did the realization of many of our possibilities and aspirations as a culture. However, along with the Airmen, having regained some recognition fifty years later, the world has been sprinkled with great African American men and women, such as Dr. Martin L. King Jr., President Barack Obama, First Lady Michele Obama, Colin Powell, and Condoleezza Rice. Now, though, more than ever, their leadership, as well as the example of others, are needed to create a greater passion for cohesiveness and prosperity, success, and power among a people who have great potential for a magnificent future.

I was once invited to speak to the ninth grade class at a predominately Jewish school. Because the Civil Rights Movement had become splintered into smaller so-called militant groups to protect against discrimination, I was to lead the class in a discussion about each group. Those young students were well-informed and participated with a good amount of knowledge of the different groups and their ideas.

After that, I was invited to speak on the same subject to a predominately black twelfth grade class at another school, using the same topics of the different militant groups. I was sorely disappointed because it seemed as though the subject was foreign to most of them.

After that experience, I wanted to know what had made the Jews so successful. Subsequently, I went to Johns Hopkins Hospital, where I believe there was somewhat of a think tank. They explained how they were planning for a gradual expansion of the hospital, located in East Baltimore. At the time, it was about eight square blocks bordering Broadway, Madison, Washington, and Orleans Streets. They said they would expand to include another educational facility besides their main campus, and redevelop most of East Baltimore. Later, Dunbar High School, my alma mater, was rebuilt in a nearby location to make room for the expansion of the hospital to the east. Currently, the hospital has been expanded to include several new services. At least until 1967, Hopkins was very discriminatory. All of my children were assigned to segregated wards after their births.

Across the street was a Jewish hospital called Sinai Hospital. It was one-third the size of Hopkins, but they would serve anyone anywhere in that little hospital. They eventually built a larger hospital in West Baltimore, which became almost as large as Hopkins.

To further understand what made the Jews so successful, I was referred to a Rabbi named Agar from a large synagogue in Northwest Baltimore. I made an appointment to meet with him, and he gave me a copy of his book. He also put me in touch with the principal of their school. He explained that they had a program in which they picked the children up from the public schools at three o'clock, three days a week. He said they believed in the public school system; they just did their own thing in the way they trained their children and encouraged them to be dedicated to their ethnic group. It served a dual purpose. It created jobs for the bus drivers who transported them and for the teachers who taught them. It also resulted in more effective management of the students' time, limiting the amount of non-productive activity, which resulted in a more disciplined and focused approach to academics, as well as effective community development. The parents were charged a stipend, and the children were allowed to run and play for half an hour and given a snack. Then they were taught history and culture.

We rightfully campaigned to teach Black History for a month rather than a week; it was time for a change. We wanted it in public schools, not only to build pride in the accomplishments of our people, but to learn about what systems and roadblocks had to be overcome for success. I vividly remember how our history was once taught with enthusiasm. When the schools became integrated, the students were taught about the accomplishments, but not necessarily about the struggles, hardships, and the real meaning of slavery. It is difficult to teach something you have not experienced, but has affected the lives and struggles of a particular culture.

After WWII, the Jewish working class dwindled. The children of these workers entered secondary schools and higher institutions of learning, and became physicians, engineers, teachers, economists, etc. Even those who remained in their old occupations, for the most part, became skilled workers and managers. The number of shop assistants and junior clerks has gradually dropped, and there are an increasingly large number of accountants, and economic and commercial directors. There are also a particularly large number of Jewish scientists in various spheres.

H.H. Ben-Hasson in "A History of the Jewish People," gives some valid points concerning discipline and methodology and stated the following:

"This process has been reflected in the activity of Jews in the life of the society around them. The number of Jews in research, technological development, mass media, literature, music, and plastic arts, far exceeds their proportion in the population or even their percentage of the urban community, to which, as in the preceding era, most Jews belong. The movement of Jews towards higher education, science, and cultural activity emerges to no small extent from their urban nature and their concentration in the

larger towns and cities. But it derives no less from the tradition of study and intellectual activity, which always characterized the Jews, and the readiness of Jewish parents, however poor, to make great sacrifices in order to provide their children with a good education. All the obstacles in the path of young Jews, such as discrimination in admission to certain American universities in the 1920s and 1930s, and the persecution in the Soviet Union during the last years of Stalin's life and sometime afterward, couldn't impede their efforts to achieve a higher education."

I remember about twenty years ago, a Jewish community requested permission to build what I believe was a school. They were denied. They elected some of their own to the governing bodies and now build whatever they want.

We blacks have a road map to improve our plight by following the process, but instead have experienced an increase in the number of gang members and arrests for various reasons. President Barack Obama cannot do it all by himself just because he is in the White House. He cannot put on a Santa Claus suit, ride in a reindeer sleigh, and give blacks gifts of gold, houses, and cars. Yes, he is one of the most brilliant presidents who ever lived; however, he cannot stop all the gangs from fighting and killing one another. He cannot pardon everyone in prison who should not have been there in the first place.

We have to be determined to be responsible and be in position to help others who cannot help themselves.

My wife, Jackie, and I have strongly agreed on several things:

1. In our house, no child of ours would have a cell phone. There was no time for gossip while trying to get an education under our roof.

2. No television was available until homework was completed and checked.

3. If a child was bad enough to go to jail, he or she stayed there.

4. There was quality pleasure and great traveling if the rules were followed.

5. Each child was bought one car to attend college.

6. We refused to buy their love or reward improper behavior.

We need to change our priorities with this generation. It was recently reported that Maryland educational institutions, Bowie State University, and Coppin State College, are numbers one and two in dropout rates in the country. Both are Historically Black Colleges. We can't keep our children in college if we don't have quality careers of our own. This will adversely affect us for many generations.

We seem to believe that if our youth get college athletic scholarships, then they will also get a good education and have a successful business career after finishing college and playing professionally. I concede we have many professional athletics earning good salaries. While young and healthy, though, this opportunity should be a means to obtain at least a master's degree, and preferably a doctorate.

When I attended Howard University, the ASTP at Hampton University, and Tuskegee Institute, I had to study three to six hours every night, including weekends. Even though I was classified as having a high IQ, I still needed all the time I could to pass. I was a fanatic in the 1960s and 1970s for the Baltimore Colts; however, we began noticing how few of the black players were involved in successful positions or owning a business. The local NAACP and members of the National Alliance got together and met with the highest officials involved with the Colts and registered our concerns. Their rebuttal was that three players had been supported in starting a business, but all three quickly failed. Another player had been given a position in communications, but was not proficient in grammar. These were athletic celebrities.

Reports indicate that schools in the poor neighborhoods are failing. During the Great Depression, we didn't have to worry about rich versus poor. All of us were poor. Now it seems as though we can't succeed in other professions, so religion is the "profession" we have come to rely on.

I know that God can call anyone to be a preacher or a pastor, but everywhere I go, there are fifteen or twenty churches, and one synagogue. The one synagogue has more power in the community than twenty churches.

Something must be done. We can't just give praise to God, have a catharsis, and then expect our children to be educated and disciplined by someone else. We should not have children we cannot afford to feed, clothe, and educate. We cannot continue to tolerate so many of our young adults filling the prisons, while leaving other children to the streets to continue the spiral into oblivion.

The Jews I have met appear to be more dedicated to community development through education. They have experienced centuries of intolerance but are committed to the "never again" position. Never again will they sit by while bigotry and evil are tolerated. Not only do they speak out against injustice, but they put their money where their mouths are.

It is my hope and prayer that blacks and Jews, both of whom have suffered cruelties at the hands of the majority, will one day demonstrate their collective strength not only to combat oppression, but also to become an example, along with the majority, of the grace, compassion, and love that Jesus championed for all humans.

JAMES O. EASTLAND, MISS., CHAIRMAN

JOHN McCLELLAN, ARK.   EVERETT McKINLEY DIRKSEN, ILL.
SAM J. ERVIN, JR., N.C.   ROMAN L. HRUSKA, NEBR.
THOMAS J. DODD, CONN.   HIRAM L. FONG, HAWAII
PHILIP A. HART, MICH.   HUGH SCOTT, PA.
EDWARD V. LONG, MO.   STROM THURMOND, S.C.
EDWARD M. KENNEDY, MASS.
BIRCH BAYH, IND.
QUENTIN N. BURDICK, N. DAK.
JOSEPH D. TYDINGS, MD.
GEORGE A. SMATHERS, FLA.

United States Senate
COMMITTEE ON THE JUDICIARY
WASHINGTON, D.C. 20510

December 5, 1967

Mr. Milton Holmes
Project Coordinator
Target City Youth Program
829 Gay Street
Baltimore, Maryland

Dear Mr. Holmes:

    I understand that the Target City Youth Program operated by the Congress of Racial Equality has completed a full year of operation, and I want to take this occasion to congratulate you. This project, funded by the Department of Labor, has made a significant contribution by training youth with criminal records to be service station attendants. This program and others like it have proven to be essential elements in the overall fight against poverty and crime.

    I wish you continued success in your efforts.

                       Sincerely,

                       Joseph D. Tydings

JDT/rjs

DR. MORRIS GELSTON
THE ADJUTANT GENERAL

STATE OF MARYLAND
MILITARY DEPARTMENT
FIFTH REGIMENT ARMORY
BALTIMORE, MARYLAND 21201

5 December 1967

Mr. Milton Holmes, Director
CORE Youth Program
832 N. Gay Street
Baltimore, Maryland 21205

Dear Mr. Holmes:

I should like to add my congratulations to the many I know you have received about the success of the training program CORE has operated.

It is my understanding that the great majority of the youths you have trained in the operation of a gas station have been employed, and with good records.

While I was Police Commissioner of Baltimore, when the plan was established, I thought it had tremendous potential. The success has borne this out.

For the benefit of the City I trust that you will find the support necessary to continue the program.

With best wishes, I am

Sincerely yours,

GEORGE M. GELSTON
Major General
The Adjutant General

MARYLAND STATE EMPLOYMENT SERVICE
DEPARTMENT OF EMPLOYMENT SECURITY
1100 N. EUTAW STREET • BALTIMORE, MARYLAND 21201 • PHONE 727-5900

OSBORNE P. BEALL
Executive Director, D.E.S.

J. DONN AIKEN
Director, M.S.E.S.

December 6, 1967

Mr. Milton Holmes
Project Coordinator
Target City Youth Program
829 N. Gay Street
Baltimore, Maryland 21205

Dear Mr. Holmes:

 We are writing to you in reference to the Auto Service Station Attendant Program which was completed on November 30, 1967.

 The objective of your program, which is to train youths as service station managers, dealers or owners, is most noteworthy. Entrepreneurship within the Negro community is not only desirable but a necessary goal which must be fostered in order to direct a large segment of our population back into the mainstream of American economic life. We were glad that we could act as co-partners with your organization in this program. Without the co-operation extended by you and your staff in the recruitment and enrollment process, the program would not have proceeded so smoothly. Your project has the distinction of being the only one in the State where the training facility has assumed the responsibility for maintaining a petty cash fund. The allowance payments to the trainees were expedited again through your assistance.

 The accomplishments of your project are a matter of the record. Unfortunately, we do not have the placement information on the project population, but we are enclosing the attached list that you forwarded to our Youth Opportunity Center for the first two classes.

 We would like to take this opportunity to commend you and your staff for the work that was done in order to make these results possible.

Sincerely yours,

J. Donn Aiken, Director
Maryland State Employment Service

Enclosure

United States Senate
COMMITTEE ON COMMERCE
WASHINGTON, D.C. 20510

December 7, 1967

Mr. Milton Holmes
Project Coordinator
Target City Youth project
829 Gay Street
Baltimore, Maryland 21205

Dear Milton:

    I want to congratulate you on a fine first year with the Target City Youth Program.

    You have made a reality of the demonstration's ideals and expectations. The vision and vitality which you have given to the project demonstrate a high degree of competence and resourcefulness.

    The people of Baltimore, the Humble Oil Company, and the Congress of Racial Equality have reason to be proud of you, and the young men you work with. I am confident you will continue to meet the daily challenges of your job with determination.

    Please feel free to call on me at any time.

    With kindest regards, I am

                    Sincerely yours,

                    DANIEL B. BREWSTER
                    United States Senator

DBB:bcg

 **POLICE DEPARTMENT ... CITY OF BALTIMORE**

FALLSWAY and FAYETTE STREET   BALTIMORE, MARYLAND 21202
Mulberry 5-1600   Area Code 301

DONALD D. POMERLEAU
Commissioner

December 7, 1967

RALPH G. MURDY
Administrative Bureau

Mr. Milton Holmes
Coordinator
Target City Youth Program
829 N. Gay Street
Baltimore, Maryland 21202

WADE H. POOLE
Operations Bureau

THOMAS J. KEYES
Services Bureau

Deputy Commissioners

Dear Mr. Holmes:

    The Target City Youth Program has rendered a real service to the citizens in our community. Due to your untiring efforts, many of our youth have been led toward a useful and purposeful goal.

    Thank you for the cooperation our Division has received from you in the past. I am certain that we will continue to have the same fruitful relationship during the coming year.

                        Sincerely yours,

                        Major William A. Harris
                        Director
                        Community Relations Division

WAH:lhl

CORE gets training aid of $147,000

A $147,000 pilot program for CORE, designed to train unemployed young men in auto service station work, has been approved by the Department of Labor.

The project will benefit 48 out-of-school youths between the ages of 17 through 21, principally in the East Baltimore anti-poverty area.

Sponsored by CORE in cooperation with the Humble Oil Co., the program will get under way soon at an ESSO station at Gay and Astor Sts.

It is to be a 12-month program, divided into two six-month sessions and combining on-the-job training with educational activities and guaranteed part-time work for the trainees.

* * *

MAJ. GEN. George M. Gelston, adjutant Maryland National Guard, was instrumental in initiating the groundwork for the project some months ago, while he was serving as Baltimore's interim police commissioner.

The Humble Oil Co. cooperated by placing four trainees selected by CORE in its retail training center in Lutherville.

These youths, having completed the course which included service station managerial training, will train those selected at the Gay St. station.

The Humble Oil Co. is also cooperating in equipping the station, and standing ready to give employment to the qualified youths who com-

(Continued on Page 18)

CORE gets

(Continued from Page 32)

plete the course.

* * *

"THERE IS a great need for qualified service station personnel," a company spokesman told the AFRO Thursday, in relating continued cooperation with the project.

He said a member of the company's personnel has been delegated in a supervisory capacity to make certain the venture is successful.

Sen. Joseph D. Tydings, who made several contacts with the Labor Department on behalf of the program, has suggested that it be watched closely, with the idea of developing it on a wider scale.

The program's stated objectives, as listed in CORE's original proposal, are to:

1. Provide educational and vocational skills necessary to operate a small business.
2. Provide information and encouragement to trainees.
3. Form business cooperatives with other trainees.
4. Improve the self-image and employability of the trainees.
5. Encourage civic and social responsibility.
6. Participate as staff or trainees in an expanded program in this area or in similar training programs.

THE SUN

Features-Fashion
Interior Decor-Art

BALTIMORE, THURSDAY, MAY 4, 1967

Youth Training Program

C.O.R.E.'s Centerpiece For Progress

By GENE OISHI

AT A tiny service station in East Baltimore a cross-eyed tiger and a snarling black panther have been harnessed together to a common purpose.

The tiger is one of Madison avenue's symbols of the fast, high-powered style of American living. The panther is the lean and hungry emblem of black power.

At the three-pump, red-white-and-blue gas station at Gay and Asquith streets, the two cats co-exist.

One urges motorists to "put a tiger in your tank."

The other is on a poster in the rear of the dingy 6-by-12-foot office. It says, "Move over or we'll move over you."

Under $121,000 Grant

The service station is operated by the Congress of Racial Equality under a $121,000, one-year grant from the United States Department of Labor.

The station is the centerpiece of C.O.R.E.'s experimental Youth Training Program, which currently has eighteen Negro youths enrolled. They range in age from 17 to 21. They are all school dropouts and most of them have prison records.

The seventeen week course is designed to train the youths as service station managers, dealers or owners.

The long-range goal, C.O.R.E. leaders say, is to nurture future entrepreneurship—the first step in developing a community of small Negro businesses, and an important ingredient of black power.

The immediate goal is to provide jobs for the youths and to give them their first look at the mainstream of American economic life.

'Resocialization'

Perhaps more important than training the youths in business management, project workers say, is the process of "resocialization" to make them see business ownership as a future possibility.

In many ways, the project resembles a Head Start project more than a dozen years delayed. The students are taken to Washington to visit their senators and congressmen, to Annapolis to see a session of the General Assembly. They are called "mister" and addressed as a group as "gentlemen."

In their turn, they learn the rudiments of business courtesy when addressing a customer: "Good afternoon, sir... Thank you, sir."

Recently, when a group of students missed some classes, Milton L. Holmes, project director, sent each a special-delivery letter, warning them in terse, businesslike fashion that they were in danger of being dropped from the rolls.

Special Request

"I told them to report to my office on Friday," Mr. Holmes said. "The letters were sent on Monday. They were in my office on Tuesday. They couldn't wait until Friday."

"They stood in my office and listened to my lecture. Then they asked me to autograph their letters. It was the first time they had received a special-delivery letter."

More important, Mr. Holmes said, the absenteeism ceased.

But that seemingly insignificant incident represents considerable progress.

When the project began last December, Mr. Holmes said, he and his staff had to comb the streets and the poolrooms to recruit the initial class of

The Big Breakthrough

"They wouldn't talk at first," he recalled. "They couldn't sit still. They resented classroom instruction, because it reminded them of their public-school experience.

"We tried to teach them Negro history and racial pride, but the big breakthrough came when we tried teaching them parliamentary procedure."

Mr. Holmes said the students took to making motions and addressing a fellow student as "Mr. Chairman." It got them talking, and involved in other class activities.

But the students learned the methods of organization only too well and that little bit of learning caused a major crisis in the project.

About ten weeks into the project, one of the instructors—a favorite with the students—resigned to rejoin the national C.O.R.E. staff in St. Louis.

"The students thought I had fired him," Mr. Holmes said. "They couldn't understand the difference between resignation and dismissal."

They Walk Out

The upshot was that all the students—there were seventeen left at the time—walked out.

"They said they were going to blow this place up," Mr. Holmes said. "They were going to shoot us all. We just said: 'Well, then I guess it's time for us to die.'"

The staff operated the service station alone for two days, as disgruntled students observed from the poolrooms, waiting for the project to fold.

Mr. Holmes said, "I sent my staff into shoot pool with them and to talk with them—not to dictate but to listen."

Eventually, a mass meeting was held in which the students aired their grievances through a spokesman. When it was over, the students agreed to return.

"They came back," Mr. Holmes said, with relief still lingering in his voice. "All seventeen of them, they came back."

Mr. Holmes considers the incident to have been one of the most positive things that grew out of this project.

"They [the students] rebelled," he said, "then they realized the leadership we had to offer and the personal commitment of each of us to make this project work."

But the crisis also developed the needed discipline.

D.C. Field Trip

About a week later, a field trip to Washington was scheduled. "I told them to be at the office at 8.35 in the morning," Mr. Holmes said. "Anyone not there at 8.35 would be left behind

"I got there a little early, but all the kids were there. Some had come at 7.15; others at 8 o'clock. At 8.35 we were off.

"We had to drive real slow. I hadn't expected to be off by 8.35 and our appointment with Senator Brewster was for 10.30."

The first class graduated in March. Its members were given a banquet prepared and served by the staff. Two youths rented a tuxedo for the occasion.

"They had never worn a tuxedo," Mr. Holmes said. "They wanted to wear one for the graduation."

Seven Dropouts

There were seven dropouts from the original class of 24. Two went to the Job Corps, one had to find a job and two quit.

Two others were suspected of stealing from service station receipts, managed largely by the students themselves. The project staff did not take any action in the case.

"The students held a meeting," Mr. Holmes said. "I don't know what they decided, but the two boys left and never came back."

Of the seventeen who graduated, ten are now employed as service-station attendants, one of them as a night manager. Two, who are mentally retarded, have been accepted in the State's vocational rehabilitation program. Five still walk the streets.

Up The Ladder Now

One of those still unemployed is a 20-year-old youth who dropped out of school after the eighth grade. He is an ex-convict, having served two years in prison after an assault and robbery conviction.

"I use to think I was nothing but a hoodlum," he said. "I think I can start going up the ladder now. I put all my heart into this program."

Project workers said there are jobs available for him. But, so far, although he continues to haunt the project offices, he hasn't asked for one.

"He'll ask when he's ready," said a

Nagged By Fear

And because of their police records, they have a constant fear of being embarrassed. One youth on his first day on the job was arrested by police who were rounding up possible suspects in a robbery case.

He was cleared of any implication in the crime, but he never returned to his job.

"I want to be a man," the students often say when they are interviewed. But manliness remains but an abstract concept for most of these youths who have never had any models.

When asked to elaborate, they roll such phrases as "being responsible," "raising a family" and "doing something for society."

Male Leadership

One youth, who served a three year prison term for burglary after being expelled from school at the age of 16, says being a man means holding a job and refraining from such "mischievious-ness" as drinking, fighting and stealing.

"That's fun, but it's kid stuff," he says.

The "Negro male," Mr. Holmes says, is still a developing concept among these ghetto youths. For that reason all nine project staff workers are Negroes, and all, except for one secretary, are male.

"We want them to respond to male leadership," Mr. Holmes says, "and he males themselves."

The students spend sixteen hours a week working in the station and sixteen hours in classes held in the project offices across the street. In addition to courses related to running a business, they learn Negro history, English, mathematics and public speaking.

They get a stipend, ranging from a minimum of $20 a week to a maximum of $64 if they have dependents.

While the money is an incentive for the youths to join the program, it is not the reason for their sticking to it, Mr. Holmes said.

"These kids could make more than that hustling in the streets," he said.

"Hustling" in this neighborhood includes gambling, snatching purses, rifling cars, burglary and even armed robbery.

351

THE SUN ARTICLE CONTINUED

Afro-American

40-Page Black Woman's Work In This Issue

AN Co., for all material previously printed in the current National Edition

BALTIMORE, MD., NOVEMBER 17, 1970 — 70 PAGES — FIVE ★ EDITION — 20 CENTS

Innis Accused Of Making CORE A Guerrilla Band

Flo can't say where all her money went

DETROIT — Ex-Supreme Florence Ballard, broke in more ways than one, is suing her former law firm for $7,500,000.

In a lengthy complaint filed in Wayne County Circuit Court, the recording artist charged members of Okrent, Baun and Vulpe, the now defunct firm with gross negligence, malpractice and breach of fiduciary duties.

Miss Ballard, now Mrs. Thomas Chapman, says she retained Rudolph Vulpe, Leonard Baun and Harry Okrent in 1967 to handle her severance from the Supremes and Motown Records.

Baun was to guide and counsel Miss Ballard on business, investments and legal questions and act as a general advisor and trustee.

She complains that Baun engaged into a $160,000 lump sum settlement with Motown and charges that this was "financially and economically unsound, since her rights against Motown far exceeded that figure.

FLORENCE BALLARD

that the law firm was not entitled to 20 per cent of a better that $90,000 savings account as part of their fee for the Motown settlement.

The complaint charges that Baun purchased and sold various shares of stock in his name with funds belonging to Miss Ballard.

In 1966, it says she was the registered owner of shares in Boeing, Magnavox, Motorola, Trans-World Airlines, American Telephone and Telegraph, Western Airlines and Zenith.

She signed a general release from her contract

The singer also alleges

Continued on page 2

31 resign from Target City unit

By AL RUTLEDGE

A control dispute over the $93,000 Half-Way House jointly run by CORE and the Target City Youth Program, Inc. has resulted in an irreparable split to threat on the life of a tween the two groups, a TCYP counselor and the issuance of a warrant for the arrest of CORE's national director, Roy Innis.

The Half-Way House was officially opened last week with many local and national figures attending the ribbon-cutting ceremony held in front of the three-story facility in the 1100 block, East Fayette.

Those present included James Farmer, former CORE chief, Mr. Innis, Baltimore Supreme Bench Judge Joseph P. Howard and other elected officials. Several talks were given but there was no mention of the CORE-TCYP rift. But TCYP officials were conspicuously absent from the group.

Hovering over the ceremony like a dark storm cloud was the current investigation being conducted by the Model Cities Board of Directors to determine if the Half-Way House should be removed from CORE

Continued on page 12

ROY INNIS

MILTON HOLMES

BLACK HISTORY MONTH

EDITOR'S NOTE: Throughout February, the Asbury Park Press is profiling black residents who have made contributions in Monmouth and Ocean counties.

It's no accident he's a clergyman

By KEITH BROWN
COASTAL MONMOUTH BUREAU

TINTON FALLS — Milton Holmes had a decision to make.

The World War II veteran and former postal worker was asked by his church pastor in Baltimore in 1965 if he would take a position as deacon. Holmes was unsure if he wanted the responsibility.

Holmes, now 79, still was pondering the decision days later while driving on a two-lane highway where two 18-wheel semi trucks, side by side, were barreling toward him just a quarter-mile away.

The oncoming trucks had both lanes blocked. There was no way to avoid a surely fatal collision. At the last minute, one of the trucks swerved slightly to the right, cre-

Rev. Milton Holmes
AGE: 79
TOWN: Tinton Falls
OCCUPATION: Former pastor, Allen Chapel AME Church, Asbury Park; community activist

ating just enough room for Holmes to squeeze his car between the two.

His decision was made. "When I got home, I was shaking like a leaf," Holmes said. "I said

See **Holmes,** Page **B2**

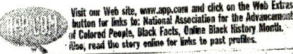

Holmes

FROM PAGE B1

'Well, that's it. I'll be a deacon.'"

He hasn't looked back since.

Holmes — Asbury Park community activist and former pastor of the Allen Chapel African Methodist Episcopal Church on DeWitt Avenue — has spent more than 30 years deepening his own spiritual connection and encouraging others to do the same.

"He's been a spiritual big brother to me," said Minister John Muhammad, a long-time friend and minister of the Respect for Life Center, a Muslim mosque based in Newark.

"He's very secure in his faith," said Muhammad of Asbury Park. "He does not have a problem meeting with Christians, Muslims, agnostics. That's a very rare thing."

A decade ago, Holmes, along with Muhammad, helped organize the Monmouth County contingent of the Million Man March, which sent more than 1,200 black men from the county to Washington.

Holmes is currently working on the committee organizing a 10-year reunion of the march involving those same men and others, which will be held later this year, Muhammad said.

Since his epiphany on a Maryland highway, Holmes has received two master's degrees and most recently a doctorate in theology from Drew University that he completed just two years ago.

Holmes cites his involvement as president of the Asbury Park Middle School Leadership Council, a advisory group of community and school leaders, as one of his chief missions.

"I think education is a key for any city," Holmes said. "I think Asbury Park could be a model city for other cities to follow. Teachers in Asbury Park are dedicated, and I think we can see real change on the horizon."

So does middle school Principal Frank Vanalesti, who said Holmes is an integral part of that positive change.

"He has had a direct impact on our school improvement process," Vanalesti said. "He's a man of high leadership caliber, and we're thankful for the great presence he has been in our middle school community. He's a gentleman of great wisdom and spirit."

While he has been heavily involved with Asbury Park, the Willow Road resident also volunteers for organizations to benefit Tinton Falls.

Holmes said he is working with the borough's Rotary Club to raise money and dedicate a gazebo for the planned West Park Avenue Park, which is a joint venture between the borough and Eatontown.

Keith Brown: (732) 643-4076 or kbrown@app.com